1 & 2 Thessalonians
Quick Study Commentary

By Chad Sychtysz

Published by
Spiritbuilding Publishers
9700 Ferry Road, Waynesville, OH 45068

1 & 2 THESSALONIANS
Quick Study Commentary
By Chad Sychtysz

ISBN: 978-1-964-80551-1

spiritbuilding.com

Table of Contents

Quick Study Commentary: 1 Thessalonians

Quick Study Commentary: 2 Thessalonians

The author of this workbook can be contacted at chad@booksbychad.com.
Cover design by Larissa Lynch

Introduction to *1 & 2 Thessalonians*

On what has been dubbed their second missionary journey (Acts 15:40–18:22), Paul and Silas sailed across the Aegean Sea from Troas to Neapolis, then traveled by land to Philippi in Macedonia. After having been illegally arrested and imprisoned in Philippi (Acts 16:22–40), they traveled through Amphipolis and Apollonia on the infamous Egnatian Way (*Via Egnatia*), and arrived at the city of Thessalonica (Acts 17:1ff)—a one-hundred-mile journey from Philippi.

Historical Background: Thessalonica was a prominent city of the Macedonians, boasting a population possibly as high as 200,000 people.[1] It was allegedly named by the Macedonian king Cassander (ca. 315 BC) after Thessalonica, the half-sister of Alexander the Great. However, some maintain that it was named after Philip of Macedon himself in honor of his victory over the armies of Thessaly. (Formerly it had been known as Therme.[2]) When Rome incorporated Macedonia as one of its official provinces in 14 6 BC, Thessalonica became Macedonia's capital city. In 42 BC, it was made a "free city," allowing it to maintain its own government and appointed political leaders as long as it did not violate the laws of Rome.

Thessalonica was also a significant commercial city strategically situated at the head of the Thermaic Gulf, a western arm of the Aegean Sea. Paul arrived there around AD 49 or 50 and sought out a synagogue of the Jews. By this time, he and Silas were joined by Timothy (Acts 16:1–3); after passing through Troas, they would also be joined by Luke (Acts 16:8ff), but Luke apparently remained in Philippi while the others continued down the Egnatian Way to Thessalonica. "And according to

---

1 Roy E. Cogdill, *The New Testament: Book by Book* (Marion, IN: Cogdill Foundation Publications, 1975), 91.

2 Albert Barnes, *Barnes' Notes*, electronic edition (database © 2014 by WORDsearch Corp.). However, P. J. Gloag in *The Pulpit Commentary*, vol. XXI (Peabody, MA: Hendrickson Publishers, no date) calls this second account "less trustworthy" than the first ("Introduction," iii).

Paul's custom, he went to them, and for three Sabbaths reasoned with them from the Scriptures, explaining and giving evidence that the Christ had to suffer and rise again from the dead, and saying, 'This Jesus whom I am proclaiming to you is the Christ [Messiah]'" (Acts 17:2–3). Linking the historical person of Jesus with the Messiah of prophecy was the cornerstone of Paul's preaching. This link was essential in demonstrating the fulfillment of God's covenant with Israel as well as the establishment of a new covenant of salvation for all people (Isa. 49:5–6, 55:3–5, etc.).

Paul's reasoning persuaded some of the Thessalonian Jews, as well as many God-fearing Greeks (likely, Jewish proselytes) "and a number of the leading women" (17:4). But other Jews resisted Paul out of jealousy and hired wicked men of the city to form a mob and make a great uproar against Paul and Silas. "The Jews were interested in making accusations against the Christians that would stand in a pagan civil court."[3] As a result of this, Paul, Silas, and Timothy determined to leave the city so as not to endanger the young church they had just established there, and they left under the cover of darkness and headed south to Berea.

Thessalonica was not the only place where Paul met resistance to his gospel. F.F. Bruce points out that "a militant messianism was spreading among the Jewish communities throughout the Roman Empire." Emperor Claudius had expelled the Jews from Rome (see Acts 18:2) because some of these were followers of a certain "Chrestus" (presumably, a corruption of "Christ"). These followers—quite possibly Christians—were allegedly the source of rioting and unrest in that city. This trouble in Rome had come from the East, and so had Paul—"carriers of what the emperor himself had described a few years earlier as 'a general plague which infests the whole world.' The fact that the rival emperor whom Paul and the others were accused of proclaiming [Acts 17:7] had been sentenced to death by a Roman judge on a charge of sedition—as anyone could ascertain who took the trouble to inquire—spoke for itself."

3 David P. Brown, "The Thessalonian Letters and Philemon—an Introduction," *Studies in 1 & 2 Thessalonians, Philemon,* Dub McClish, ed. (Denton, TX: Valid Publications, 1988), 20.

Paul's preaching of Jesus, which included His ultimate return as a universal Judge of all the earth, could have easily been interpreted as a rival emperor or king. Given this, not to mention the jealousy and opposition of the unbelieving Jews themselves, it is not hard to see how the Thessalonian city officials interpreted the situation as something that had to be suppressed immediately.[4] The tenacity of these Jewish opponents of the gospel, however, is evidenced in the fact that they followed Paul into Berea in order to drive him out of Macedonia altogether (Acts 17:13–15).

Purpose and Theme: When Paul finally arrived in Athens, Greece, he sent Timothy back to Thessalonica to see how the church there was weathering the strain of persecution (1 Thess. 3:1–5). Paul had moved on to Corinth by the time Timothy returned to him, bearing good news about the Thessalonian Christians' faithfulness and determination. Yet Timothy also brought reports of concern over their misunderstandings concerning the Second Coming of Christ and the physical resurrection. Paul decided to write a letter to the church to offer encouragement as well as correct teaching on these subjects.

First Thessalonians may be the first (surviving) epistle that Paul wrote; *2 Thessalonians* may be the second.[5] Both epistles appear to have been written close together in time, perhaps within a few months of each other. Most scholars agree that the date of writing is ca. AD 51–52, during Paul's eighteen-month-long stay in Corinth.[6] There is virtually

---

4 F. F. Bruce, *Word Biblical Commentary, vol. 45: 1 & 2 Thessalonians* (Nashville: Thomas Nelson, Inc., 1982), "Introduction," xxiii–xxiv.

5 "We cannot say that this is Paul's first letter to a church, for in II Thess. 2:2 he speaks of some as palming off letters as his and in II Thess. 3:17 he says that he appends his own signature to every letter after dictating it to an amanuensis [secretary—MY WORD] (Rom. 16:22). We know of one lost letter (1 Cor. 5:11) and perhaps another (II Cor. 2:3). But this is the earliest one that has come down to us and it may even be the earliest New Testament book, unless the Epistle of James antedates it or even Mark's Gospel" (A. T. Robertson, *Word Pictures in the New Testament,* vol. IV [Grand Rapids: Baker Book House, no date; © 1931 by SBC], 3).

6 An old subscription appended to the epistle in the KJV read, "The First Epistle to the Thessalonians was written from Athens." This has since been proved to be a mistake and cannot be taken seriously. "These subscriptions at the end of the Epistles have no

no dispute that Paul is the author of both epistles. This conclusion has also been attested by Irenaeus, Clement of Alexandria, Tertullian, Gaius, and Origen—early church "fathers" who quoted from these letters and attributed them to Paul.[7]

The church at Thessalonica was one of the jewels of Paul's ministry. This group of believers listened to the message of salvation, followed it with great enthusiasm, and weathered great difficulty in defense of it. Paul speaks glowingly of these people, boasting about their "work of faith and labor of love and steadfastness of hope" (1 Thess. 1:3). While the city of Thessalonica was full of idols and idolaters, the Christians there had turned from that vain lifestyle to "a living and true God" (1 Thess. 1:9), which gave Paul great reason to rejoice over them.

In the first epistle, Paul reminds these Christians of how tenderly and patiently he worked with them. This provides an example of how they also are to deal with those who initially resist their sharing of the gospel with others. Just as Paul remained humble and compassionate in his ministry to them, so they must exercise these same virtues toward others. He informs them that it has been his earnest desire to return to them but has been hindered by his own work and Satan's interference (1 Thess. 2:17–20). Thus, he sent Timothy as his personal ambassador—a man to whom Paul refers elsewhere as his "kindred spirit" (Phil. 2:20).

In the fourth chapter of *1 Thessalonians*, Paul begins giving instructions and teachings rather than mere exhortations and explanations of his situation. He emphasizes holiness of conduct, especially sexual purity (since immorality was commonplace in pagan cities of the ancient

---

authority; and although in general correct, yet occasionally, as in the present instance, they are erroneous" (Gloag, "Introduction," viii).

7 Robert Jamieson, Andrew Fausset, and David Brown, *Jamieson, Fausset, and Brown Commentary: Commentary Critical and Explanatory on the Whole Bible (1871)*, electronic edition (database © 2012 by WORDsearch Corp.), "Introduction to 1 Thessalonians"; Brown, "An Introduction," *Studies*, 26. See also William Hendriksen's involved analysis on the authorship of these epistles (*New Testament Commentary: Thessalonians, the Pastorals and Hebrews* [Grand Rapids: Baker Books, 1995], 18–30.

world). He then provides some of the most important (albeit brief) teaching in the New Testament (NT) on the Second Coming of Christ and the resurrection of the righteous. Since the specific *day* of Christ's coming cannot be determined—only the *suddenness* of it—Paul strongly admonishes these people to live in readiness for that event. He then provides a series of brief but potent exhortations that are consistent with a people preparing themselves to greet the Lord upon His return.

Second Thessalonians seems to have been written shortly after the first epistle. It does not appear that Paul (or his fellow ministers) had visited Thessalonica between the writing of the first and second epistles to the church there.[8] Nonetheless, he must have received reports of serious misunderstandings concerning his original teaching on the Second Coming; or, there were some who were providing false information on this subject, disturbing the minds of some believers (2 Thess. 2:1–2). Apparently, some Thessalonian Christians assumed that Jesus would be returning at any moment; in response to this, they had quit their jobs and made themselves dependent upon fellow believers while they awaited this event.

Paul strongly rebukes this action and orders these people to get back to work and stop imposing upon others: "If anyone is not willing to work, then he is not to eat, either" (2 Thess. 3:10). Paul "commands" that the Thessalonians obey his instruction on this matter; they are to remove from fellowship those who refuse (2 Thess. 3:14). Thus, despite his high regard for this group of believers, Paul has admonished them with some of the strongest language found in any of his epistles.[9]

---

8 It is not even conclusive, in the minds of some Bible scholars, that *2 Thessalonians* was the *second* epistle to this church and not the first. The arguments in support of this appear to be unconvincing, but F.F. Bruce (for one) does spend some time in his commentary providing the details of this question ("Introduction," xl–xliv). Personally, I am convinced that the order in which they appear in the NT is also the order in which they were written.

9 A parallel to this is found in Jesus' rebuke of Peter (Mat. 16:21–23). Even though Peter was one of Jesus' closest friends on earth, the Lord called him "Satan"—something He never said even to the Pharisees who had given Him such grief and later conspired to execute Him.

In this second epistle, however, Paul also provides two unique (and intriguing) teachings on Christ's return. First, he explains that Christ "will be revealed from heaven with His mighty angels in flaming fire, dealing out retribution to those who do not know God and to those who do not obey the gospel" (2 Thess. 1:7–8). This provides information not given in the first epistle concerning the circumstances of that future event. Second, he speaks of a mysterious "man of lawlessness" (or "son of destruction") and the deceptions with which he will usher in a great apostasy (i.e., falling away from the faith) (2 Thess. 2:3–12). The Second Coming of Christ will not take place until this "man of lawlessness" comes first and runs his full course. This provides more contextual information than we had before on this subject. Unfortunately for us, he told the Thessalonians more about this in person than what he wrote in his letter.

General Outline of *1 Thessalonians*

- ❑ Salutation and Opening Remarks (1:1–10)
- ❑ Paul's Care for the Thessalonians (2:1–12)
- ❑ Paul's Praise for Their Faithfulness (2:13–20)
- ❑ Timothy's Visit to Thessalonica (3:1–13)
- ❑ Sanctification and Love (4:1–12)
- ❑ The Gathering of the Saints (4:13–18)
- ❑ Anticipation for Christ's Return (5:1–11)
- ❑ Practical Conduct and Final Remarks (5:12–28)

General Outline of *2 Thessalonians*

- ❑ Salutation and Opening Remarks (1:1–12)
- ❑ The "Man of Lawlessness" (2:1–12)
- ❑ Commendation and Admonition (2:13–3:5)
- ❑ Dealing with the "Unruly" (3:6–15)
- ❑ Final Remarks (3:16–18)

The First Epistle to the Thessalonians

Salutation and Opening Remarks (1 Thess. 1:1–10)

This salutation (1:1) is quite typical of Paul's other epistles. "Paul" is Christ's hand-picked spokesman (Acts 9:15–16), "called as an apostle, set apart for the gospel of God" (Rom. 1:1), and a "bondservant" of Jesus Christ (Phil. 1:1). "Silvanus" is the Romanized (Latin) name for Silas, one of Paul's trusted traveling companions (Acts 15:36–41) and fellow prisoner in Philippi (Acts 16:16ff). "Timothy" is Paul's young protégé who had joined him in the middle of Paul's second missionary journey (Acts 16:1–3). He is the same (relatively) young man to whom the epistles of *1 & 2 Timothy* are addressed.

Paul's having included Silvanus and Timothy in the salutation does not imply that these men share his authority as an apostle; rather, they are both familiar to and concerned for the church at Thessalonica. Paul is clearly the writer of this letter and it carries the weight of his apostolic authority in all matters for which this is necessary.

"To the church … in God the Father and the Lord Jesus Christ" (1:1)—usually, Paul says, "church *of* God" rather than "in God." Yet, this expression "designates God and Christ as the sphere in which the church exists," and is thus parallel to the many forms of "in Christ" that Paul uses in his epistles.[10] In any case, while the Father and Christ remain distinctly different Personages of the Godhead, they are both "God" and are both the object of every believer's faith.[11]

10 Bruce, *WBC*, 7.

11 Both the Father and the Son (Christ) are Divine Personages; they, along with the Holy Spirit, comprise the Godhead, or simply "God." This triune God is all-powerful, all-knowing, eternal in nature, and self-existent; by contrast, all other life—whether in heaven or on earth—has been created and is upheld only by the power and sovereign authority that God alone possesses. For more detail on this, I recommend my exposition on Col. 1:15–18 in *Philippians, Colossians and Philemon Commentary*; go to www.spiritbuilding.com/chad.

Faith, Love, and Hope (1:2–5): Paul prays constantly for the Thessalonians (1:2–4), no doubt asking for the same things that he asked on behalf of the Colossians: knowledge, spiritual wisdom, the ability to please God and bear fruit for Him, strength, perseverance, patience, and joy in their inheritance (cf. Col. 1:9–10).[12] Instead of mentioning *what* he prays for in this case, he refers instead to *why* he prays: these people are hardworking Christians who are facing a very difficult situation (to be discussed shortly). Three things capture Paul's attention: their work of faith, labor of love, and steadfastness (or, cheerful endurance) of hope in God.

- **"work of faith"** does not separate work *from* faith but unites the two concepts into one. Whatever a person does for God *in* faith is a work *of* faith. Everything a Christian does for God is a work of faith, since he offers his service to a God whom he has never seen, a Christ he has never met, and for a reward he cannot even comprehend. "Although Paul never substituted *works* for *faith*, the passage here shows that the two go together; and it may therefore be accepted as gospel that when Paul mentions *faith* in the NT, it never means anything other than an obedient, working faith."[13]
- **"labor of love"** accurately (but uncommonly) illustrates the true nature of one's love [Greek, *agape*] for the Lord. Such love is neither carefree nor toil-free; it is not always enjoyable or comfortable; and it always demands self-sacrifice to one degree or another. Christian love, when rightly practiced, is *challenging work*, yet these Thessalonians are obviously not afraid this. Yet, difficult as such love is, it is also a godly virtue and the most fulfilling way to live. This deeply impresses Paul, and he freely praises them for it.
- **"steadfastness of hope"** indicates a hope in God *and* a concurrent

12 "It would seem that the missionaries [i.e., Paul, Silas, and Timothy—MY WORDS] prayed *unitedly* (in addition, of course, to praying individually). They may have taken turns in leading the devotions. These prayers were not marked by any vagueness. On the contrary, the needs of the various churches were mentioned one by one, as the occasion demanded. The thought is not excluded that individual members may have been mentioned by name" (Hendriksen, *NTC*, 46).

13 James B. Coffman, *Commentary on 1 & 2 Thessalonians, Titus, and Philemon* (Austin, TX: Firm Foundation, 1978), 11–12; emphases are his.

hope in one's future with God that is not wavering, vacillating, or filled with doubt. It is easy to "hope" in something during times of peace and comfort; it is far more difficult to keep one's hope alive amid struggle, conflict, and persecution. Yet, when this hope is real and firmly grounded, it will carry a believer through the most difficult of situations (Rom. 5:3–5). The Thessalonians' hope is "in our Lord Jesus Christ": it is based upon His willingness and ability to fulfill it. Those without God are also without hope (Eph. 2:12).

"In the presence of our God and Father" (1:3) refers primarily to Christ's proximity (for lack of a better word) to the Father, being at His right hand (Acts 2:33, Col. 3:1, etc.). Yet Paul implies that the Thessalonians' faith, love, and steadfastness have the Father's full attention.

"Knowing, brethren beloved of God, His choice of you" (1:4) is one of those phrases Calvinists eagerly cite in support of their Doctrine of Predestination. This doctrine states that God alone chooses the salvation (or, by default, the condemnation) of every person before he is even born; no one can fall from his "election" or protest his "reprobation" because God's sovereign decision cannot be questioned. Yet, Paul says nothing in his epistles to support such teaching. Whenever he uses the words "choice," "choosing," or "elect" with reference to Christians, he means them in a *collective* context, not a singular one. In In other words, such passages speak of the "choice" of a group of Christians—and often, the entire body of Christ (as in Eph. 1:3–5)—rather than the predestination of one person's eternal destiny.

The word "predestination" in Scripture does not mean what Calvinism claims it means. It is true that God predestined the establishment of the Thessalonian church; or, we could say that God predestined the church of Christ, and these Thessalonian Christians have become members of that church. It is not true that God had already decided the eternal future of each Christian at Thessalonica before he or she was born. This latter view violates the purpose of Christ's preaching, the apostolic ministry, the need for the gospel and its proclamation, and the free will of every person.

It is God's will that *all* human souls be saved (1 Tim. 2:4); Jesus came to "seek and save the lost" (Luke 19:10), not those who are allegedly already saved. God's gospel is proclaimed to all people, and every person who hears it decides independently whether he will obey it. "All who of their own volition believe and obey the Gospel of Jesus Christ are elected of God simply because they have complied with the terms He instituted in His own mind before the world began, and which, by His Gospel, have been made known unto man."[14]

The "power of the Holy Spirit" validated the authenticity of the gospel message that Paul preached to the Thessalonians (1:5). This likely has a dual reference. On the one hand, it most certainly refers to the demonstration of miracles which Paul performed to prove that his message was indeed from God (2 Cor. 12:12, Heb. 2:3–4, etc.). On the other hand, it can also refer to Jesus' fulfillment of the Old Testament (OT) scriptures to prove that He was indeed the Messiah/Christ of prophecy (Acts 17:1–4). Both the prophecies *and* the earthly ministry of Christ were the work of the Holy Spirit. Such was God's part in confirming the message to these people.

"With full conviction" (1:5) refers to Paul's part in in the matter: he did not come to them as a charlatan seeking a gullible audience, but with sincerity and integrity, and without an ulterior motive. Paul and company did not only preach the gospel of Christ, but they also lived it; they did not only speak the truth, but they also walked according to that same truth (cf. 3 John 3–4). Paul, Silvanus, and Timothy "proved" what kind of men they were by their own conduct, not just by the words they spoke. As Jesus taught, a "tree [i.e., one's true character] is known by its fruit [the visible expression of that character in words and deeds]," not only by what it professes itself to be (Mat. 12:33, bracketed words are mine).

"For your sake" indicates the selfless motive of this sincere preaching: it was not to trumpet Paul's personal humility or his speaking abilities (see 1 Cor. 2:1–5), but to provide the Thessalonians with God's truth which leads to salvation (cf. Eph. 1:13–14).

14 Oran Rhodes, "Paul's Salutation and Thanksgiving," *Studies*, 55.

The Thessalonians' Excellent Example (1:6–9): "You also became imitators of us and of the Lord" (1:6)—because Paul's conduct imitated Christ, he also was worth imitating (1 Cor. 11:1, Phil. 3:17, 2 Thess. 3:7–9, etc.). Not only should *mature* Christians be worth imitating, but those who are *new* to the gospel ought to imitate them (Heb 13:7). Christ ("the Lord") is the standard by which all exemplary behavior is measured, however. Anyone who offers himself as an *example* of the Lord must also live in a manner consistent with His own conduct (1 John 2:4–6). If he does not do this, then neither should anyone follow him (cf. 1 Cor. 14:37–38). The present passage, however, does not emphasize Paul's good conduct but the Thessalonians' excellent example. Paul is not on trial; it is the Thessalonian Christians who are under examination. Thankfully, they have exhibited a Christ-like attitude and behavior with all sincerity and genuineness.

However, the Thessalonians did not receive the word of God in a vacuum, devoid of all opposition. Instead, they have "received the word in much tribulation" (1:6). From the very beginning, Paul's preaching incited a great deal of resistance (Acts 17:4–9); it is apparent that the church in Thessalonica continued to experience this resistance even after his departure. This refers to those Jews who saw the gospel of Christ as a threat to the Law of Moses and their own prestige within the city.

Nonetheless, the Christians saw past this "tribulation" [lit., distress, persecution, or trouble[15]] and embraced instead "the joy of the Holy Spirit"—a joy derived from living in harmony with God's Spirit. For this reason, they "became an example to all the believers in Macedonia and in Achaia" (1:7)—i.e., throughout the entire region of ancient Greece. (These two Grecian provinces had been recognized separately since 142 BC.) In other words, the church at Thessalonica serves as a model church for the rest of the brotherhood.[16] This does not imply that they are

15 Strong, *Dictionary* (electronic), G2347.

16 "A joyfully suffering church in Thessalonica meant exceedingly much for believers elsewhere, who in most cases also had to face vicious opposition. We see the broadness of Paul's view. The steadfast joy of one church means so much for others. When we suffer, let us think not only of ourselves but also of all the others whom our joy in endurance may aid" (R. C. H. Lenski, *Commentary on the New Testament: The Interpretation of Paul's Epistles to the Colossians, to the Thessalonians, to Timothy, to Titus,*

without fault or error in understanding; yet they are striving to achieve the ideal standard of what Christ intended.

"For the word of the Lord has sounded forth from you" (1:8)—i.e., wherever people talk about your faith, they also talk about what your faith is based upon: "the word of the Lord." Thus, the godly faith of this church serves as a kind of preaching of the gospel. "They had not actually gone out themselves, but their story and reputation were repeated by Christian merchants of Thessalonica who traveled widely."[17] "So that we have no need to say anything"—i.e., Paul does not have to convince others of the genuineness or faithful obedience of the Thessalonian church, but their reputation has already preceded them (and his own testimony). This does not mean Paul says nothing at all about them; he is proud of this congregation and takes every opportunity to boast about them (as he did with others—see 2 Cor. 9:1–2, for example). It does mean, however, that whether Paul says anything, people know who the Thessalonian Christians are and what they stand for.

Specifically, what is known of the Thessalonians is that they "turned to God from idols to serve a living and true God" (1:9). This indicates not a superficial change or a simple transition, but a complete transformation of beliefs, character, and moral responsibility. Previously, these people were pagans who worshiped false gods, partook of immoral practices, and behaved as heathens. Yet, in doing so, they had no real virtues, no atonement for sins, and no hope for a (happy) afterlife. Their spiritual beliefs were predicated upon gods that could not act, speak, save, or prove anything. Non-living gods cannot impart life to anyone, no matter how devoutly one believes in them.[18] In sharp contrast, the "living and true God" is:

---

and to Philemon [Peabody, MA: Hendrickson Publishers, 1998], 230).

17 JFB, *Commentary* (electronic), on 1:8.

18 Paul's words are made even more remarkable when we remember that Thessalonica was a pagan city filled with idolatry, and that Mount Olympus, the alleged home of the pantheon of Greek gods, was a mere 50 miles to the south of this city.

- ❑ **self-existent and self-sufficient.** His power or existence does not depend upon the adoration of those who follow Him; likewise, it is not compromised by those who do not. Even if every Christian in the world turned against Him and denounced his faith in Him, God remains as alive, powerful, and perfect as He ever was.
- ❑ **"living"** ***and*** **can impart life to others.** He is the source of life; no one lives apart from His power; no one operates outside of His authority (Isa. 44:8, 1 Cor. 8:4–6, etc.).
- ❑ **"true."** In Him there is no lie (Titus 1:2), "shifting shadow" (James 1:17), or darkness (1 John 1:5). "This is the message we have heard from Him and announce to you, that God is Light, and in Him there is no darkness at all" (1 John 1:5).[19]
- ❑ **dependable.** This is the necessary implication of His being both *living* and *true*. God will not disappoint those who believe in Him (Rom. 10:11), even if such belief brings about tribulation or persecution. This God—and no other—is *worth* believing in, no matter what the cost of that belief. This is what the Thessalonians proclaim through their own actions. Whether one hears their preaching, their actions speak loudly enough.

Christ's Second Coming (1:10): "And to wait for His Son" (1:10) — this refers to the return of Christ, also known as His Second Coming. This event is often referred to by commentators as the *Parousia* [lit., "Coming" or "Advent"], the word literally used 1 Thess. 5:23 ("coming").[20] The Thessalonians seem preoccupied with this subject, which Paul himself mentions several times throughout both epistles to them, but they also misunderstand some of its details. Christ's death, burial, and resurrection on the one hand, and His Second Coming on the other, serve as the two bookends of the believer's faith. In faith, the believer looks back to what *has* happened; in faith, he also looks forward to what *will* happen. The Lord's Supper memorial links these two events: in it, all believers "proclaim the Lord's death [a historical fact] until He

19 For a study on "the Light" and "the darkness," I strongly recommend my book, *This World Is Not Your Home* (Spiritbuilding Publishers, 2022); go to www.spiritbuilding.com/chad.

20 "This is the only place in the Thessalonian letters where Jesus is called the Son of God" (Bruce, *WBC*, 19).

comes [a future promise]" (1 Cor. 11:26, bracketed words added). Thus, we "wait" with anticipation, but we cannot determine how long this wait will be.

Christ will come "from heaven [or, from the heavens]" to which He ascended when He left this world (Acts 1:9–11) and in which He presently dwells (Col. 3:1). "[W]hom He raised from the dead"—there is no mistaking who will return: it will be the same One who resurrected from the grave. Christ overcame death, took His seat "in the heavens" (Heb. 8:1–2), and promises to return for His saints (Heb. 9:27–28). Thus, Paul unites the three events—Christ's resurrection, His ascension, and His return—as being the grand triad of the Christian faith.[21]

"[Christ is He] who rescues us from the wrath to come" (1:10)—the Christian's salvation is not a promotion based upon personal merit, nor an entitlement based upon status or favor. Instead, it is a rescue mission led by Christ Himself, and we who are rescued by *His* own power are helpless to save ourselves by *our* own power (Cor. 1:13–14). Contrary to modern attempts to diminish or dismiss it altogether, God's "wrath"—His settled anger toward the disobedient—is real and cannot be explained away. He will demonstrate His divine wrath against His enemies in time. In every discussion about "salvation," it is God's *wrath* from which we are *saved* (Rom. 5:8–9).

In a politically correct society that puts far more weight on feelings and personal offenses than on divine authority and moral righteousness, "wrath of God" sounds jarring and inappropriate. Many believe that God is only about love, tolerance, acceptance, and non-judgment; a God that deals out wrath and punishment is inconsistent with their version of the God of the NT. (This immediately overlooks all that God did in the *Old* Testament.) Yet it is God Himself, through His revealed word, who repeatedly informs us of His wrath toward sin and those who practice it.

21 "The hope of the second coming of Christ was real and powerful with Paul as it should be with us. It was subject to abuse then as now as Paul will have to show in this very letter. … He is certain that God's wrath in due time will punish sin. Surely this is a needed lesson for our day. It was coming then and it is coming now" (Robertson, *Word Pictures*, 14).

Consider the following sample passages (bracketed words are all mine):

- "He who believes in the Son has eternal life; but he who does not obey the Son will not see life, but the wrath of God abides on him" (John 3:36).
- "For the wrath of God is revealed from heaven against all ungodliness and unrighteousness of men who suppress the truth in unrighteousness" (Rom. 1:18).
- "But because of your stubbornness and unrepentant heart you are storing up wrath for yourself in the day of wrath and revelation of the righteous judgment of God" (Rom. 2:5).
- "to those who are selfishly ambitious and do not obey the truth, but obey unrighteousness, [God will show] wrath and indignation" (Rom. 2:8).
- "Much more then, having now been justified by His blood, we shall be saved from the wrath of God through Him [Christ]" (Rom. 5:9).
- "Let no one deceive you with empty words, for because of these things the wrath of God comes upon the sons of disobedience" (Eph. 5:6; see Col. 3:6).

We must be careful not to embrace the world's soft-pedaled depiction of God. Rather, we are to accept whatever God says about Himself, whether we or others are comfortable with this or not.

Paul's Care for the Thessalonians (1 Thess. 2:1–12)

This chapter opens with Paul's return to his earlier comments about his personal conduct among the Thessalonians (2:1). His noble conduct reflects the sincerity and integrity of his preaching: it was earnest, productive, and true. "[W]as not in vain" according to the Greek tense of "was" indicates an ongoing action, as in, "it continues to not be vain." What Paul began with the Thessalonians continues to produce beneficial results and is personally rewarding to him. Paul expresses his brotherly relationship with these people in the frequent use of the term "brethren" throughout this epistle.

Paul's Own Shameful Suffering (2:2): The suffering and mistreatment in Philippi (2:2) refers to Paul and Silas' unlawful beating and imprisonment in that city (Acts 16:22–40).

> The *shame* of the treatment consisted in the fact that it was wholly undeserved; that it was contrary to the laws; and that it was accompanied with circumstances designed to make their punishment as ignominious as possible. The Thessalonians knew of this, and Paul was not disposed to palliate the conduct of the Philippians. What was 'shameful treatment' he speaks of as such without hesitation. It is not wrong to call things by their right names, and when we have been abused, it is not necessary that we should attempt to smoothe [*sic*] the matter over by saying that it was not so.[22]

Immediately after having left Philippi, Paul and Silas had gone to Thessalonica, so the Thessalonian Christians became familiar with the news of that situation, in part because of Paul's personal testimony of it. (It is likely, too, that his body still showed the actual scars and effects of that beating.) No doubt he reminds them of this to give perspective to their own suffering and mistreatment. In effect, he says, "I know you are going through a serious ordeal for your faith—remember how I also had suffered for this same reason" (see 2 Tim. 1:8, 12, and 3:12). Yet, despite the suffering, Paul showed boldness in his faith by continuing to preach the gospel in Thessalonica, even though he suffered there as well. "Opposition" means conflict, struggle, or striving. In other words, the gospel is a message of *contention* with those who resist it, yet a message of *salvation* to those who receive it (cp. Mat. 10:34–36 and 1 Cor. 1:18).

The Sincerity of Paul's Preaching (2:3–6): Paul clarifies (again) that his preaching of the gospel was not: false information (in error); corrupted (impure), or motivated by evil (deceitful) (2:3). "Exhortation" [Greek, *paraklesis*] comes from the same root word from which "advocate" (1 John 2:2) and "helper" (John 14:16) are derived. In a sense, Paul says, "We comforted you *not* with a false sense

22 Barnes, *Barnes' Notes* (electronic), on 2:2.

of comfort or a disingenuous message," but brought a message of hope and consolation instead. "So many wandering charlatans made their way about the Greek world, peddling their religious or philosophical nostrums, and living at the expense of their devotees ... that it was necessary for Paul and his friends to emphasize the purity of their motives and actions by contrast with these."[23]

Rather than seeking to please men—in particular, by preaching a man-made doctrine—Paul delivered to them a gospel entrusted to him by God Himself (2:4). God approves of Paul by the fact that He appointed him to be a minister (or steward) of His Son's gospel (Rom. 1:1, Gal. 1:15–16, Col. 1:25–27, etc.). The "we" reference does not undermine Paul's personal authority as an apostle; God also approves of Silvanus and Timothy, even though they do not share his authority or responsibility. "[N]ot as pleasing men, but God who examines our hearts" is another way of saying, "We did not speak to impress you, but—and God Himself will testify to this—came to you with the purest of intentions" (see 1 Cor. 4:1–4). God is the One who determines the righteousness of a person's intentions or motives, not oneself or other men.

The phrase "flattering speech" [lit., with a word (*logos*) of flattery] is a unique expression in the NT (2:5). (Paul expounded upon this thought in 1 Cor. 2:1–5.) Paul did not court the favor of men but sought to convey God's truth without any false pretense. "The meaning is, that the apostle did not deal in the language of adulation; he did not praise them for their beauty, wealth, talent, or accomplishments, and conceal from them the painful truths about their guilt and danger."[24]

Paul also was not motivated by the prospect of financial gain ("greed") as were those who "peddled" the word of God for money (2 Cor. 2:17). Those whose only motive for preaching is to make money will say whatever must be said to get paid; it matters little, in such a case, whether the information is true, helpful, or sincere. Paul interjects here "God is

---

23 Bruce, *WBC*, 26.

24 Barnes, *Barnes' Notes* (electronic), on 2:5.

witness"—i.e., he is not hesitant to call upon God Himself to testify on his behalf.

Again, Paul maintains that he did not "seek glory from men" (2:6a), since this would have compromised the message (Gal. 1:10–12). For a contrast of this, see John 12:42–43, where some of the Pharisees put their desire for the approval of men above their acceptance of Christ. Such men "have their reward in full" (Mat. 6:1–5). Sadly, this same selling out of one's allegiance to Christ for the sake of human praise or peer approval is not hard to find today.

"Even though as apostles of Christ we might have asserted our authority" (2:6b)—that is, we could have simply *commanded* you to obey the gospel, but we *appealed* to you instead. Paul uses "apostles" in the most general sense here (as in Acts 14:14), as "one sent (with a message)" and not a hand-picked representative of Christ (as in Acts 2:42 or 8:18). The phrase "asserted our authority" means "made ourselves a burden to you (by imposing upon you)." Its connection to the previous thoughts implies a *financial* burden, as in, "We could have insisted that you pay us for our services (because it was worthy of remuneration), but we chose not do so."[25]

Paul constantly struggled with people's perception of compensation: he was willing to preach to a new group without compensation from them (1 Cor. 9:14–15), but some took this to mean that his gospel was not worth anything. At the risk of this latter perception, Paul nonetheless reminds the Thessalonians that he did not request money from them while he was with them; however, he did receive support from others (Phil. 4:16).

Motherly Affection and Fatherly Guidance (2:7–12): "But we proved to be gentle among you" (2:7): Paul's treatment of the Thessalonians was not only genuine but also extremely considerate. "Gentle" does not mean soft (as in weak), timid (as in apprehensive), or unsure (as in lacking confidence), but *mild* in character, as opposed to being

25 Adapted from JFB, *Commentary* (electronic), on 2:6.

disrespectful, over-bearing, or insensitive. "As a nursing mother … her own children" does not imply effeminacy on Paul's part. Instead, he simply compares the demeanor he showed to the Thessalonians with that of a mother's care for her infant child: gentle, patient, forbearing, and selfless. This is evident not only in how he, Silas, and Timothy conducted themselves among them, but also in what they *imparted* to them (2:8). Just as a mother has something to give to her infant child, so Paul gave the gospel to these people.

"But also our own lives" has a twofold sense: first, Paul (as well as others) *risked* his life to preach the gospel among the hostility of the Jews; second, he *devoted* his life to the preaching of the gospel. Either sense is correct here. "Because … dear to us"—i.e., you [Thessalonians] made the risk worthwhile because of your own excellent response. This calls to mind Paul's words in *Romans*: "For one will hardly die for a righteous man; though perhaps for the good man someone would dare even to die" (Rom. 5:7). It seems fair to say that Paul was willing to die, if necessary, to bring the gospel to the Thessalonians.

Paul then reminds these Christians of specific characteristics of his (and Silas' and Timothy's) actual conduct among them (2:9):

- **"our labor and hardship"**—likely, this refers to the work of preaching and teaching in general. Anyone who has engaged in the work of full-time "preaching and teaching" will testify that it involves "labor and hardship" to one degree or another. JFB translates this as "weariness and travail."[26]
- **"working night and day"**—in essence, doing whatever it takes to cover his needs and expenses. It is safe to assume that Paul refers here at least in part to his self-employment as a tent-maker (Acts 18:3). Besides his own self-generated income, he was also helped by financial contributions from the church at Philippi.
- **"we proclaimed to you the gospel of God"**—Paul threw himself tirelessly into this effort, and considers it a work unto itself (Acts 20:31). This proclamation (or, preaching) was not an easy task, but consumed Paul's time and attention.

26 JFB, *Commentary* (electronic), on 2:9.

Paul then describes the *manner* of his conduct among them—"devoutly and uprightly and blamelessly"—and then evidences of that behavior—"exhorting and encouraging and imploring" (2:10–11a). Not only can the Thessalonians attest to Paul's earnest actions, but so can God; his motives are transparent, pure, and honorable. The sincere and righteous manner of his conduct complements the integrity and soundness of the message that he preached. A necessary part of this preaching, however, includes personal encouragement to *do what is right* (as in 1 Peter 3:10–16) as well as a sense of urgency to do this right thing *now*.

Paul earlier compared himself to a mother's treatment of her infant child. Now he compares himself to a father's handling of his (older) son in impressing moral responsibility and providing exhortation to walk uprightly (2:11b). The two comparisons are not equal; the age of the child (in either analogy) changes the emphasis on the point Paul is making. A mother cannot treat her older son like an infant, and a father cannot impart moral responsibility to an infant. The point is not that the Thessalonians were infantile or behaving like actual children, but (by comparison) were new to the gospel and had to be taught the fundamentals of faith before moving onto more difficult subjects.

And what does Paul, in the role of a "father" to these people (see 1 Cor. 4:15), need to say to them? "[I implore you to] walk in a manner worthy of the God who calls you" (2:12a). He has said similar things to other Christians elsewhere:

- "Only, as the Lord has assigned to each one, as God has called each, in this manner let him walk. And so I direct in all the churches" (1 Cor. 7:17).
- "But I say, walk by the Spirit, and you will not carry out the desire of the flesh" (Gal. 5:16).
- "Therefore I, the prisoner of the Lord, implore you to walk in a manner worthy of the calling with which you have been called" (Eph. 4:1).
- "Brethren, join in following my example, and observe those who walk according to the pattern you have in us" (Phil. 3:17).

- "walk in a manner worthy of the Lord, to please Him in all respects, bearing fruit in every good work and increasing in the knowledge of God" (Col. 1:10).
- "Therefore as you have received Christ Jesus the Lord, so walk in Him" (Col. 2:6).

The instruction to "walk" in a worthy manner necessarily implies three things.

- **First**, this "walk" is doable and expected: Paul is not asking for a hypothetical, figurative, or metaphorical thing, but a real and visible demonstration. It is not a mere apostolic suggestion but an apostolic command.
- **Second**, this "worthy manner" is known to those who are to walk in it. Paul is not saying, "You figure out how to walk, and whatever you come up with will be 'worthy' if you feel sincere about it." Such seems to be the general "me first" theology today that masquerades as genuine Christianity. Rather, Paul has told these people how to walk, and this information describes the *only* "walk" of which God approves.
- **Third**, if there is a worthy manner, then anything different than this is *unworthy* and must be rejected (cf. 1 Cor. 11:27). Such language is inclusive and exclusive: it includes all who walk as Paul instructed; it excludes all who walk in any other manner.

"Who calls you into His own kingdom" (2:12b)—in nearly every case after Acts 2, "the kingdom" is something into which a believer *anticipates* entering (as a promise to be fully realized in the life to come), whereas "the church (or body)" is something into which he enters *immediately* (as a real state of being).[27] All Christians must be in Christ's church; they cannot be Christians otherwise. Ideally-speaking, all Christians must also subject to the kingdom of God since the church is the sanctuary of

27 The rare exception, such as in Col. 1:13, can be explained by a change in how the "kingdom" is understood, not as a contradiction to this thought. There, Paul is not using "church" and "kingdom" interchangeably—he does not even mention the church—but focuses entirely on one's *allegiance* to one Lord (Christ) or another (Satan).

believers within this realm of Christ's authority over all things. But the Christian's relation to the kingdom has to do with his present *subjection* to, and not his permanent *entrance* into, that kingdom. For example, consider the following passages:

- "[Paul and Barnabas were] strengthening the souls of the disciples, encouraging them to continue in the faith, and saying, 'Through many tribulations we must enter the kingdom of God'" (Acts 14:22, bracketed words are mine). These men are speaking to people who are *already* in Christ's church (a finished action) about something that remained unfulfilled (a promised event).
- "Or do you not know that the unrighteous will not inherit the kingdom of God? Do not be deceived" (1 Cor. 6:9). The Corinthians had already been baptized into Christ's *church*—this was unquestionable (1 Cor. 12:12–13)—but they had yet to enter the glory of God's eternal *kingdom*—this was dependent upon their continued faith. Those who refuse to seek Christ as their Savior "will not inherit" this ethereal kingdom: they are unprepared to do so, having never been cleansed by the blood of Christ.
- "Now I say this, brethren, that flesh and blood cannot inherit the kingdom of God; nor does the perishable inherit the imperishable" (1 Cor. 15:50). Obviously, all Christians who are on earth presently are in Christ's church, but—because we remain in the flesh—we cannot yet enter God's eternal kingdom.
- "envying, drunkenness, carousing, and things like these, of which I forewarn you, just as I have forewarned you, that those who practice such things will not inherit the kingdom of God" (Gal. 5:21). Notice the future tense of this entrance.
- "For this you know with certainty, that no immoral or impure person or covetous man, who is an idolater, has an inheritance in the kingdom of Christ and God" (Eph. 5:5).
- "This is a plain indication of God's righteous judgment so that you will be considered worthy of the kingdom of God, for which indeed you are suffering" (2 Thess. 1:5). No one can enter the God's kingdom until God deems him "worthy"—by his *faithfulness*, not his meritorious works.

- ❑ "The Lord will rescue me from every evil deed, and will bring me safely to His heavenly kingdom; to Him be the glory forever and ever. Amen" (2 Tim. 4:18). Paul was most certainly in Christ's church, but he had not yet entered the kingdom of God. He was *promised* this—just as all Christians are promised this—but the promise had not yet been *realized* or completed.
- ❑ "for in this way the entrance into the eternal kingdom of our Lord and Savior Jesus Christ will be abundantly supplied to you" (2 Peter 1:11). If you are "in Christ," then this speaks of an accomplished action: you obeyed Christ's gospel and as a result He added you to His church. But your "entrance into the eternal kingdom" requires that you add to your faith, live out that faith in earnest, and remain faithful till death (Rev. 2:10). Otherwise, you will be *denied* that kingdom [necessarily implied].

In each of these examples, "the kingdom" is not something already received, but something yet to *be* received (or inherited). Christians are "in" the kingdom now as a matter of promise (as heirs or sons of God), but this promise is contingent upon our remaining faithful to that which we were called. In other words, if we walk in the manner of those who *are* heirs, we will indeed inherit that which God promised us. Christians are *presently* in Christ's church, but this present association with Christ will only last as long as we remain faithful to the head of that church. When the church itself is ushered into glory—having been purified of those who chose *not* to remain faithful to Christ—then we will receive our full inheritance, and the promise will be completely and visibly fulfilled.

Paul's Praise for Their Faithfulness (1 Thess. 2:13–20)

The Thessalonians' Reception of the Word of God (2:13–16): "For this reason" (2:13a)—i.e., so that the Thessalonians might walk as Paul had instructed them. Amid his instruction on *what* to do, Paul often intersperses a reason or purpose for *why* it is to be done. He did not conduct himself in a certain manner for nothing; he had a noble objective in mind, and he expected God-fearing men and women to respond rightly to his efforts—and especially to his God-given message. When Paul preached the word of God among them, they accepted it as such; they did not resist it (like the unbelieving Jews did) or reduce it to just another version of fanciful religion (like the Athenians did—Acts 17:16–21).

The "word of God" here is synonymous with the "word of truth" (Col. 1:5), "message of truth, the gospel of salvation" (Eph. 1:13), or "sword of the Spirit" (Eph. 6:17). It is the "living and enduring" good news that must be known ("preached") to be believed (1 Peter 1:23, 25). The "word of men" is of human origin and a corruption of the truth. Such messages may *sound* like the "word of God" but do not have its power and cannot replace it (Gal. 1:6–7). "The word of human beings, however wise in substance or eloquent in expression, cannot produce spiritual life: this is the prerogative of the word of God, which works effectively in believers."[28]

In contrast, God's word "performs its work in you who believe" (2:13b)—i.e., it *does* something that could not have been done otherwise. It teaches, examines the human heart, evaluates one's beliefs, penetrates to the deepest core of one's being (Heb. 4:12), and forces a conviction from everyone who hears it. The Thessalonians obviously believe in this word and its power since they submit to its teaching and are willing to suffer persecution for it (2:14).

In this way—through both obedience *and* suffering, not one or the other—these Christians followed the example of the Judean churches that have endured these same things (1 Peter 5:9). "Your countrymen" means "one of the same people,"[29] and in this case it means the Macedonians in general, but the Jews in particular. The faithful Jewish Christians in Jerusalem (or Palestine) provide a precedent to their own actions. In other words, what they did was exactly what other noble-minded people have done.

28 Bruce, *WBC*, 45.

29 Joseph Thayer, *Thayer's Greek-English Lexicon*, electronic edition (database © 2014 WORDsearch Corp.); G4853.

Paul's characterization of the Jews who persecute Christians is bold yet accurate (2:15–16). These men plotted—to the extent that God allowed—the execution of Jesus (Mat. 20:18, 26:4, 27:1, John 11:47–53, Acts 2:23, etc.). This is one of the only places in all his writings where Paul holds "the Jews" personally responsible for Jesus' death. (The only other place is in 1 Cor. 2:6–8.) They and their ancestors also killed "the prophets," which can refer to the ancient prophets as well as those who preached the gospel of Christ (Mat. 23:29–36). "[A]nd drove us out"—the Jews had literally forced Paul out of Thessalonica (Acts 17:5–10); but they also forced him out of other cities as well (Acts 13:50, 14:1–2).

"They [i.e., the unbelieving Jews] are not pleasing to God, but hostile to all men" (2:15)—they are not pleasing to God because they refuse to listen to Him; they are hostile to all men because they hinder (or, put a stumbling block in the path of; poison the minds of) those who hear the gospel preached to them (Mat. 23:13, Acts 14:1–4). "The worst feature of unbelief is not its own damnation but its effort to frustrate the salvation of others."[30]

Even though the Jews consider themselves God's people, their rejection of Christ and His followers proves otherwise. Jesus called them children of the devil (John 8:44), and He called their churches synagogues of Satan (Rev. 2:9, 3:9). They believe that persecuting Christians and killing them find favor with God, when in fact such hostility only compounds His condemnation against them. Paul should know: in thinking that he was acting with God's approval, he once viciously attacked Christ and His church (Acts 26:9–11).

"They always fill up the measure of their sins" (2:16) is an expression that Jesus used in this same context (Mat. 23:32). It refers to (their) choosing to let their sinful behavior run its full course, and thus completely justifying God's punishment of them (Gen. 6:13, 15:16, Jer. 16:18, Amos 2:6ff, Rev. 18:4–6, etc.). They are doing now, Paul says, what they have always done; it is their established character to resist God and act on their own impulses (Acts 7:51–53). "Their hindrance

30 Lenski, *Interpretation*, 267.

of the Gospel preaching to the Gentiles was the last measure added to their continually accumulating iniquity, which made them fully ripe for vengeance."[31]

"But wrath has come ... utmost" (2:16)—the Greek is in the past tense here, indicating that divine punishment has already begun to manifest itself upon the Jews. Paul is not specific here, and we might be inclined to think that any trouble the Jews faced at this time in history is part of a divine judgment.[32] One scholar interprets this as: "They have reached the point of no return in their opposition to the gospel and final, irremediable retribution is inevitable; indeed it has already come."[33] One thing is clear: when God's divine vengeance against Israel *did* come, it was as evident as lightning in the sky (Mat. 24:15–28). This was fulfilled in the Romans' complete destruction of Jerusalem in AD 70.

We should not misunderstand Paul's disposition toward his countrymen, the Jews. He loves them and seeks their best interest (see Rom. 9:1–5 and 10:1–4, for example), but he also knows that the Jewish *nation* is under a divine curse. The wicked action of those who murdered Jesus and persecuted Christians only serves to justify such a curse. It was Jesus Himself who pronounced this curse upon the nation—as a final declaration for the cumulative effect of centuries of rebellion against God—for rejecting the visitation of their King (Luke 19:41–44).

Thus, Paul is not speaking spitefully here, or with gleeful anticipation of the Jews getting what is theirs, so to speak. At the same time, the Jews have been the *most privileged people on the planet* for having been the sole recipients of a covenant with God *and* for having His Son walk through their cities and teach them in person. "From everyone who has been given much, much will be required" (Luke 12:48).

---

31 JFB, *Commentary* (electronic), on 2:16.

32 JFB, for example, mention that a riot in Jerusalem (in AD 48) resulted in the deaths of 30,000 Jews (*Commentary* [electronic], on 2:16). This may be an example of God's judgment against that people; or it may be simply another sad event in human history. We can speculate either way—and sometimes we may well be right—but we cannot know for certain.

33 Bruce, *WBC*, 48.

Paul's Hope, Joy, and Crown (2:17–20): Paul abruptly shifts from the dark and heavy talk about God's enemies to the positive and joyous subject of the Thessalonian believers (2:17). While Timothy may have remained for a while in that city, Paul (as well as Silas) was "taken away" from them, but not by choice. It was in their best interest for him to leave Thessalonica, since his presence there was the primary reason for the Jews' hostility.

> It was very probably represented by the enemies of Paul and his fellow-labourers [*sic*], that they had fled from Thessalonica on the slightest danger, and had no regard for the church there, or they would have remained there in the time of peril, or, at least, that they would have returned to visit them. Their continued absence was probably urged as a proof that they had no concern for them. The apostle meets this by stating that they had been indeed "taken from them" for a little time, but that their hearts were still with them, and by assuring them that he had often endeavoured [*sic*] to visit them again … [34]

Since then, however, he has wanted to return to them in person, "and yet Satan hindered us." This likely refers to the same hindrance he had just mentioned (in 2:16), which Satan himself incites (2 Cor. 4:3–4). Or it could refer to a different incident or circumstance that Paul did not disclose. It is unlikely—but not implausible—to think that Paul is referring to his "thorn in the flesh" which he characterized as a "messenger of Satan" (2 Cor. 12:7). "Us" indicates that Satan targeted all three of the preachers (Paul, Silas, and Timothy), not Paul alone.

"For who is our hope or joy or crown …?" (2:19–20)—i.e., Paul wants them to know with certainty that he has been prevented from returning to them because of things beyond his control, and not for any other reason. He thinks very highly of these people—he has spent two chapters so far telling them this!—and has no personal reason to avoid them or delay his visit with them. He also implies that when Jesus comes, Paul will (so to speak) point to the Thessalonians as a showcase

34 Barnes, *Barnes' Notes* (electronic), on 2:17.

of his own preaching—i.e., he will boast about them to the Lord, since they believed the message he spoke among them (2 Thess. 1:10).

At (or near) the end of every chapter in this epistle, Paul makes mention of Christ's return. (In 2:19 is the first actual use of the word *parousia*, the "coming" of Christ, in the Greek text of this epistle.) This future event is a predominant part of his teaching, and not a rarely mentioned subject (as is often the case today). While the Thessalonians certainly misunderstood certain aspects of this Second Coming, Paul does not shrink back from underscoring the *certainty* and *finality* of the event itself. "For you are our glory and joy"—Paul highly valued these people; they are a hallmark of his apostolic ministry.

Timothy's Visit to Thessalonica (1 Thess. 3:1–13)

If we piece together information from Acts 17–18 and this account, the following scenario emerges:

- Paul and Silas arrived in Thessalonica from Philippi. Timothy either accompanied them or joined them shortly thereafter (possibly bringing financial support for Paul from Philippi).
- A mob uproar forced Paul and Silas to leave Thessalonica; Timothy appears to have remained behind for a short time.
- Paul and Silas traveled to nearby Berea; Timothy joined them later.
- Unbelieving Jews from Thessalonica came to Berea to upset the work of Paul and Silas. Paul was forced to leave and went to Athens. Silas and Timothy remained for a while in Berea but apparently joined him in Athens. After having little success in Athens, Paul went to Corinth; Silas and Timothy remained for a while in Athens (until Timothy was sent back to Thessalonica—see below), then joined him. Paul remained in Corinth for a year and a half.

Paul Explains What Happened (3:1–5): "We thought it best to be left behind at Athens alone" (3:1) refers to when Paul, Silas, and Timothy were together in Athens. The "we" refers to Paul and Silas, who decided to send Timothy back to Thessalonica to encourage the brethren there;

this forms the background of 1 Thess. 3. The three evangelists would rejoin in Corinth, which they did (Acts 18:5). Paul grieved over having to abandon the Thessalonians, and—while it was impractical for him to return there himself—sent Timothy to them. Timothy is Paul's protege, and obviously a very capable young man. Paul calls him his "kindred spirit" (Phil. 2:20), a man after Paul's own heart. Timothy is the next best thing to Paul's own presence. Here, Paul calls Timothy "our brother and God's fellow worker in the gospel of Christ" (3:2a)—a more practical and factual description, yet highly commendable.

Timothy's purpose was to "strengthen and encourage" the faith of the Thessalonian believers (3:2b). The specific need for this strengthening and encouraging centers upon their concern for Paul (and company) having to endure physical persecution for preaching the gospel (3:3a).[35] In other words, it bothered them deeply to see this happening, just as it would bother anyone today to watch a fellow believer suffer for his faith. Implied in this is, of course, concern for their own suffering, and the negative effect it could have upon their young faith—a concern toward which Paul was very sensitive. "We have no report as to what happened after Paul and Silvanus left the city [of Thessalonica], but we can be quite sure that the opposition continued to the distress of the Thessalonians."[36] Thus, Timothy's visit was meant to comfort them, so that they would not abandon the gospel for fear that it was more trouble than it was worth.

"For you yourselves know that we have been destined [or, appointed] for this" (3:3b)—i.e., such afflictions are a natural expectation of preaching the gospel amid those who violently oppose it; "Indeed, all who desire to live godly in Christ Jesus will be persecuted" (2 Tim. 3:12). What happened to Paul—and what *will* happen to him—should have been no surprise to the Thessalonians, since Paul predicted it before they ever saw it with their own eyes (3:4). Being forewarned, "they should have

35 "The word rendered 'moved' [Greek, *saino*, translated "disturbed" in the NASB] occurs nowhere else in the New Testament. It properly means to wag, to move to and fro, as of dogs which wag their tails in fondness … ; then to caress, to fawn upon, to flatter; then to move or waver in mind-as from fear; to dread, to tremble" (Barnes, *Barnes' Notes* [electronic], on 3:3; bracketed words are mine).

36 Lenski, *Interpretation*, 285; bracketed words are mine.

also been forearmed."[37]

"For this reason" (3:5)—Paul returns to his original thought (from 3:1) to finish the explanation. The only change here is that he changes the "we" to "I"—or, from a shared view to his personal one. He sent Timothy to learn of the state of the congregation's spiritual well-being (their "faith"), "for fear that the tempter might have tempted you." The only natural identity of "the tempter" is Satan (Mat. 4:3), who works through false teachers who have succumbed to his deceptions (2 Cor. 11:13–15). Paul's fear is that these false teachers will have an intimidating and convincing sway over the Thessalonian believers' tender faith, and thus they would yield to such men and abandon their confidence in Christ.

"And our labor ... in vain"—a practical concern, but well-justified. Paul had put a great deal of time and effort to bring the gospel to Thessalonica—especially if we consider the rigors of the entire second missionary journey itself. More importantly, he did not want all those who had turned from idolatry to a "living and true God" (recall 1:9) to abandon Him for a different form of idolatry than what they had to begin with (i.e., self-justification by works of law). Elsewhere, he has expressed this same concern: "But now that you have come to know God, or rather to be known by God, how is it that you turn back again to the weak and worthless elemental things, to which you desire to be enslaved all over again? ...I fear for you, that perhaps I have labored over you in vain" (Gal. 4:9, 11; see also 1 Cor. 15:1–2 for a parallel thought).

Timothy Brings Refreshing News (3:6–10): "But now that Timothy has come to us from you" (3:6–8)—this refers to Timothy having joined Paul in Corinth, after having already gone to Thessalonica. It is at this point that Paul sits down (in Corinth) and writes this epistle to the Thessalonians. He cares deeply for these people, and obviously they care deeply for him. Timothy has brought good news, and this has refreshed Paul's worried mind: "for now we really live"—lit., we are among the living; our souls have been revived. At the same time, he understands that not all the danger has passed since what first threatened their faith

37 JFB, *Commentary* (electronic), on 3:4.

will attempt to do so again. Thus, he is glad for the good news ("we were comforted about you"), but then there is the admonition ("if you stand firm in the Lord").

"Stand firm" is one of Paul's trademark expressions used throughout his epistles (1 Cor. 16:13, Gal. 5:1, Eph. 6:10–14, Phil. 1:27, etc.). The phrase has a military connotation, as in, "Stand your ground" or "Do not desert your post" in the face of adversity or the enemy (cf. Heb. 10:36–39). It also is used in contrast to *stumbling* or *falling* in a spiritual context, as in falling away from the faith (2 Peter 1:10, Heb. 3:12). Paul is saying to the Thessalonians, "I am greatly refreshed by the news of your faith! But do not relax your efforts for a moment, for the enemy is relentless."

Even so, Paul rejoices in the report he has received from Timothy and continues to pray for their spiritual welfare. In due time, he has every intention of returning to Thessalonica in person (3:9–10), which he will do several years later on his third missionary journey (Acts 20:1–2).[38] His intention is "to complete what is lacking in [their] faith"—i.e., to impart to them whatever teaching, encouragement, and spiritual help that he, as an apostle of Christ, can uniquely provide (Rom. 1:11, 2 Cor. 13:9). Their beliefs were not altogether accurate (or mature), and Paul wanted to correct this.

Appeal for Divine Help (3:11–13): "Now may our God…and Jesus our Lord direct our way to you" (3:11)—while it was Paul's intention to return to Thessalonica, he allows the Lord to make the actual decision. Paul makes his plans, but things do not always happen this way.[39] "And … increase and abound in love for one another" (3:12)—because

38 Two Christian men from Thessalonica—Aristarchus and Secundus—accompanied Paul on his mission of mercy to Jerusalem (Acts 20:4). Aristarchus would also accompany Paul on his ill-fated voyage to Rome and may well have been imprisoned alongside of him (Acts 27:2, Col. 4:10).

39 In Acts 16:7, Paul and Silas sought to go into the province of Bythinia, "and the Spirit of Jesus did not permit them." In Rom. 15:28, Paul had every intention to sail to Spain after delivering the contributions of the Gentile churches to the church in Judea, but he was arrested in Jerusalem and spent the next several years in various prisons, awaiting his rightful day in court.

no claims of faith or discipleship are worth anything without genuine demonstrations of godly love (John 13:34–35). Christian love must be always increasing; it ought never to plateau or diminish.

"So that [the Lord] may establish your hearts without blame in holiness" (3:13a): to have one's heart "established" is to have it purified, strengthened, and consecrated to God. It is God who establishes the believer (2 Cor. 1:21–22, Heb. 13:20–21); no Christian can be "self-established," "self-reliant," or self-*anything*. Everything we do *as* Christians is directly and necessarily dependent upon the sound teaching, moral guidance, and spiritual strength that God provides. If this is not so, then we do not need God to be Christians, we can achieve holiness on our own, and all the references to standing strong "in the Lord" are meaningless.

"At the coming of the Lord Jesus with all His saints" (3:13b)—yet another reference to the Second Coming. (The details of this event are covered in the commentary on 4:13–17.) "Saints" comes from the Greek *hagios*, meaning "holy ones." This can (and often does) refer to Christians in the NT (Acts 26:10, 1 Cor. 1:2, Rom. 1:7, etc.), but in scenes of glory and judgment God (or Christ) is depicted as being surrounded by angels. Thus, some have concluded that Paul could have meant "angels" here; or he means both angels and those who have died in the Lord (cf. Rev. 14:13). Suffice it to say for now: "It is not safe, under any circumstance, to postulate any detailed description of what will take place at the Second Coming of Christ, because the glimpses afforded of that event in the NT are not full reports, but only glimpses, given here and there, of that glorious and terrible morning when all men will be summoned before the great white throne for their accounting before the Lord of all creation."[40]

40 Coffman, *Commentary*, 42.

Sanctification and Love (1 Thess. 4:1–12)

Excelling Still More (4:1–2): "Finally then" (4:1)—this is another occasion (like in Phil. 3:1) where Paul thinks his epistle is nearing completion, yet he has much more to say. His strong admonition to the Thessalonians is that they "walk" and "please God" according to the instructions that he had given while he was still with them. "Walk" refers to a habitual lifestyle, behavior, or conduct; it conveys the idea of steady, rhythmic, and consistent activity. To "please God" is to keep His commandments, honor His Son, and serve fittingly as His representative. It is a general instruction, but not one to be taken lightly.

In Mic. 6:8, we have an example of another general-yet-very important instruction: "He has told you, O man, what is good; and what does the LORD require of you but to do justice, to love kindness, and to walk humbly with your God?" These passages are over seven hundred years apart yet speak of the same virtuous behavior that God expects of His people. The difference is that, in Paul's case, "the Lord Jesus" provides a specific role model for such excellent behavior.

When he says, "excel still more," Paul is not insinuating that the Thessalonians are slipping in their "walk"; he admits just the opposite. Yet, there is still room for improvement, as there will always be in the case of human effort. This is a critical point: here is a congregation doing well yet is still capable of *doing even better*. To "excel" [lit., to abound; to be over and above][41] does not imply a passive interest in what a person (or group) is doing, but an earnest, active, and purpose-driven one.

> The Thessalonians are to please God in a still higher degree. Not only is perfection still unattained, [but] there are faults that are of a kind that ought to disappear completely. The Thessalonians have for the greater part come out of rank paganism and have not at once shaken off all pagan ideas and practices.[42]

41 Thayer, *Lexicon* (electronic), G4052.

42 Lenski, *Interpretation*, 305; bracketed word is mine.

This can be said of all of us who have come out of the world and into Christ. At first glance, however, Paul appears to be saying, "Great job! But you still need to do better." Such a takeaway leaves the reader deflated, thinking that "No matter what I do or how good I do it, it's never good enough for God!" This is not at all what Paul means. He is not *diminishing* his praise of their behavior by *increasing* their moral responsibility. Rather, he is saying, "Keep abounding in what you have been doing already; you are growing well but you are not *done* growing." It is an admonition to *stay the course* rather than a criticism that *they haven't done enough.*

> Herein lies the great burden of excelling still more. How well we remember the triumph of successfully tackling that one persistent sin, or learning to genuinely love that seemingly unlovable person. But those wins are simply milestones, not the destination. Not even close. There remains yet another sinful deed to put to death, another attitude to bring into submission, another thought to take captive, another Christian to learn to love, another unbeliever, another enemy. We have before us a race to run that constantly demands that we "excel still more." Is it any wonder some give up?[43]

No one can "walk" in Christ *or* please God, however, who does not follow the pattern revealed by God through His apostles (4:2). We cannot violate or disregard the divinely revealed pattern while claiming to honor the One who *gave* us the pattern.[44] F. F. Bruce writes: "The apostolic tradition is not to be treated indifferently; it is to be accepted because it is the tradition of Christ, by whose authority the apostles deliver it."[45] Contemporary, "progressive" religion that self-identifies as "modern Christianity" seems oblivious to this. Doctrinal instruction

---

43 Andy Cantrell, "Excel Still More," *A Life Worthy of the Gospel: Studies in the Macedonian Epistles*, Florida College Annual Lectures (2023), Jason S. Longstreth, ed. (Temple Terrace, FL: Florida College Press, 2023), 40.

44 For a study of this "pattern," I strongly recommend my book, *The New Testament Pattern: God's Plan for Christians and Their Churches* (Spiritbuilding Publishers, 2023); go to www.spiritbuilding.com/chad.

45 Bruce, *WBC*, 79.

is set aside in favor of popular beliefs, social causes, and feel-good activities. Regardless, God's call (through Paul and his gospel) to walk according to the divine commandments still stands and will last for as long as the earth remains.

A Call to Sexual Purity (4:3–8): Paul's particular concern is for the Thessalonians' *sanctification*, which refers to the act or process of being set apart (or made holy) to God (4:3–8). These people have converted from a pagan culture in which idolatry and sexual immorality are common and expected; indeed, they still live amid that society. It would be easy for them to slip back into old behaviors, or to combine old habits with their new life in Christ and call this mixture "Christianity."

Paul reminds them, then, that they no longer belong to themselves but to God. It was God's *will* that they be set apart to Him; it is also God's will that they *remain* in this condition and not allow carnal lusts to compromise it. "Sexual immorality [or, fornication]" is a general expression with broad applications. It comes from the Greek *porneia,* from which we get "pornography," and refers to any illicit sexual activity, including premarital sex, adultery, incest, "and things like these" (Gal. 5:19–21). Regardless of how or why the Macedonian society condones fornication, this activity remains sinful behavior in God's sight. Since this is true, there can be no justification for it among believers.

> Sexual immorality is still rampant in our world and sadly at times in the body of Christ. This kind of behavior is not pleasing to God. It is sinful in nature. Nothing good will ever come from it. The devil wants us to think that sexual immorality is where we will find pleasure and satisfaction, but it will only bring about regret, pain, terrible consequences, and separation from our God.[46]

Paul then is more specific in his comments: "that each of you know how to possess his own vessel in sanctification and honor" (4:4). Some want "vessel" to refer to the control of one's own body, and there is certainly an appropriate understanding of this (1 Cor. 6:19–20). Yet "possess"

46 Benjamin Lee, "Walk Worthy of the Gospel," *A Life Worthy,* 107.

(in the Greek) never means "control," but refers to an acquisition of something—in this case, a wife.[47] Thus, Paul says "You need how to acquire a wife in a righteous manner—and continue your relationship with her in this same manner."[48] Paul wrote a parallel thought in 1 Cor. 7:1–2: "It is good for a man not to touch a woman. But because of immoralities, each man is to have his own wife, and each woman is to have her own husband."

Fidelity to a monogamous marriage between a man and a woman provides the Christian with the proper context for his sexual needs. "Not in lustful passion" like those who remain in spiritual ignorance, not having been enlightened by divine influence (4:5). "The Graeco-Roman world did not demand sexual purity of men."[49] Indeed, the ancient world looked indifferently upon prostitution, temple prostitution, concubines, and mistresses. (There was certainly a double standard: women did not have the same freedoms as men to do these things and remain respectable.[50]) Yet, God demands that His people not act like those of the sinful world: "'Come out from their midst and be separate,' says the Lord. 'And do not touch what is unclean; and I will welcome you. And I will be a father to you, and you shall be sons and daughters to Me,' says the Lord Almighty" (2 Cor. 6:17–18).

Paul continues his thought: "that no [Christian] man transgress and defraud his brother [in Christ] in the matter" (4:6; bracketed words

47 Thayer, *Lexicon* (electronic), G2932. The *idea* of exercising control over one's own body certainly is biblical (as in 1 Cor. 6:19–20), but the context here indicates something different than this. The decision between the two ("wife" or "body") hinges on the actual meaning of "possess." It should be noted that commentators are nearly equally divided between the two positions.

48 "Paul speaks of acquiring a wife, i.e., entering upon marriage, and not of the conduct of marriage; when it is entered into in the right way, marriage will be conducted in the right way" (Lenski, *Interpretation*, 310).

49 JFB, *Commentary* (electronic), on 4:5.

50 "The double standard for the two sexes was taken for granted. Married men were allowed a freedom which was out of the question for married women. … [However,] moderation in sexual activity, as in other forms of indulgence, was proper to a civilized man" (Bruce, *WBC*, 87). Yet, there must not be any double standard for the Christian: "When the husband comes to the marriage bed, he should come as a chaste man to a chaste wife" (Robertson, *Word Pictures*, 29).

added). The context dictates the understanding of this thought: Paul is speaking specifically of one Christian sexually violating the "vessel" of another—a woman who is either betrothed or married to his brother in Christ. (This can equally apply to a Christian woman who violates the husband of a fellow sister in Christ.) The *transgression* is against God; the *defrauding* is against his fellow believer; *both* actions are condemned.[51] "[I]n the matter" likely refers to the context of marriage, or anticipation of it.[52]

"The Lord is the avenger in all these things"—i.e., whether the act of fornication is discovered, God knows of it completely since "all things are open and laid bare to the eyes of Him with whom we have to do" (Heb. 4:13; see also Rom. 2:16), and He will punish those who practice such things (Heb. 13:4). God has not "called" men and women into fellowship with Him so that they can behave like those who remain *outside* of this fellowship. He did not make us holy (i.e., sanctify us) so that we could continue in impurity, like those still under condemnation (see 1 Peter 1:13–16).

Whoever rejects this instruction—namely, by engaging in the very things that he forbids—not only violates Paul's authority, but opposes God Himself, since His Spirit is the authority behind Paul's words (4:8; cf. 1 Cor. 14:36–38). In other words, there can be no legitimate rationalization for the kind of behavior of which Paul warns in this passage.

Their Love of the Brethren (4:9–12): These warnings having been given, Paul now gives attention to other matters—some of which the Thessalonians are very capable, and others in which they need to

---

51 The Greek word used here for "transgress" (*huperbaino*) is unique to the NT, and indicates the crossing of a boundary, in this case a forbidden one, "and hence trespassing (sexually) on territory which is not one's own" (Bruce, *WBC*, 84; see also Thayer, *Lexicon* [electronic], G5233).

52 Some commentators see Paul as having changed the subject here from sexual purity to purity in business or commerce, so that the "defrauding" has to do with cheating or swindling someone in a business transaction. While it is certainly true that Christians must never be cheaters or swindlers, there seems to be little justification for such a conclusion in this particular passage (see Hendriksen, *NTC*, 101–102).

improve. The phrase "love of the brethren" [Greek, *philadelphia*] refers specifically to the family-like concern and respect that Christians ought to have for one another, since we all are brothers and sisters in the body of Christ (4:9–10). The Thessalonians know what this means, for they have been taught it correctly and practice it well—not only toward their own group, but also toward Christians outside of their group ("in all Macedonia").

> [The Thessalonian Christians] loved being together. They were emotionally knit together like a quilt; each patch sewed to another until they made a masterpiece. They were a body where every member needed every other member for the strength and health of the whole. They were a building where every brick was required to provide stability. They were a flock, where every sheep mattered, and none would rest until all were safe within the fold.[53]

Even so, while their conduct is commendable, Paul again implores them to "excel still more" (4:10). While they have acted admirably, there is always room for improvement, and there are still higher levels of growth, understanding, and proficiency. Godly love is not something that anyone masters and then has no further need of instruction or demonstration of it; instead, it is a learned behavior, and we are forever learning it.

Furthermore, Paul expects these brethren to lead a "quiet" and industrious life that does not impose upon (or cause trouble for) others (4:11). No doubt this refers to reports he has received (likely, from Timothy) that some Thessalonians have abandoned their jobs and other responsibilities and are sitting around waiting expectantly for Christ to return at any moment. There is no doubt that He will return—Paul has said so several times already—but this is no reason to abdicate all responsibilities in the meantime. It is also improper for Christians to impose upon *other* Christians (for food or other necessities) because of such unwise and avoidable decisions. (This first epistle did not, however, correct the problem entirely; in the second epistle, Paul will be more forceful in this instruction.)

53 Adam Shanks, "Taught by God to Love One Another," *A Life Worthy*, 160.

Christians are to set an example of steady, productive, and wholesome behavior—at home, on the job, in society, and in all their relationships. We are to "lead a tranquil and quiet life in all godliness and dignity" (1 Tim. 2:2). We also have a moral obligation to "behave properly toward outsiders"—i.e., those who are not Christians (see Col. 4:5)—and not unnecessarily make ourselves a financial burden to others or to the church (4:12). To do otherwise brings reproach upon God and the church (Titus 2:6–8).

God expects His people to be busy with their hands, working for a living, and industrious (1 Thess. 4:11, 2 Thess. 3:12, etc.). This includes domestic work as much as a secular job or career (1 Tim. 5:14, Titus 2:5, etc.). Christ's church, likewise, is meant to be filled with workers, laborers (of the kingdom), teachers, preachers, evangelists, and shepherds. In Rom. 16:3–12, for example, Paul identifies several Christians as "workers," "fellow workers," and those who have "worked hard in the Lord." Elsewhere, he says that hardworking elders are to be esteemed for their efforts and are worthy of "double honor" (i.e., extra remuneration) (1 Thess. 5:12–13, 1 Tim. 5:17–18). When people are not busy working, they are "busy" doing something else—often, something that they are not supposed to do (2 Thess. 3:11, 1 Tim. 5:13). A "troublesome meddler" (1 Peter 4:15) is someone with way too much time on his hands and who uses this time to interfere with the lives and work of others.

The Gathering of the Saints (1 Thess. 4:13–18)

It is obvious that Paul taught about the Second Coming of Christ while he was in Thessalonica, due to references to it so far in this epistle. But an event as fascinating and unique as this is also subject to misunderstandings and misinterpretations—and the Thessalonians certainly have these. One misunderstanding addressed in this section is the question of what the state of those who have already *died*. Will these people miss the Lord's return? Will they see otherworldly glory—or is there "no hope" for them? Such questions might appear self-evident to us, but only because we are blessed with hindsight *and* the written record of what Paul explained to these people.

This entire passage (4:13–18) is one of the clearest and most insightful of all the passages dealing with Christ's return. Even so, it remains limited in its explanation. Paul does not provide a detailed account of this event, nor is this necessary to understand its basic outline. Many questions remain, even after reading this—questions that the Holy Spirit has chosen not to answer. What is clear: the resurrection of believers is a *real* and *future* event. (If there is no resurrection, then our faith is in vain—1 Cor. 15:12–19. If it has already happened, then *we ourselves* will have "no hope" of participating in it—2 Tim. 2:16–18.) Furthermore, this will not be a "spiritual" resurrection, or merely a symbolic or figurative one, but a *literal* raising of bodies from the grave. The focus here, however, is on one aspect of Christ's Second Coming—namely, what will be the *order* of events in His grand appearance?

The Status (When Christ Returns) of Christians Who Have Died (4:13–14): "[T]hose who are asleep" is a euphemism for the dead, or the figurative state of being of those who have died (4:13). Jesus (John 11:11–14) and Paul (1 Cor. 15:6, 51) used this terminology elsewhere, and the OT writers used it numerously (1 Kings 2:10, 11:43, 14:31, etc.). "So that you will not grieve as do the rest who have no hope"—i.e., there is *no hope* to save friends and family members once they have died outside of the Lord. The same can be said of the ones who have died: *they also* (now) have a conscious knowledge that they have "no hope."

Thus, Paul contrasts "no hope" with those who *have* hope—those who *have* died in the Lord (Rev. 14:13) or those faithful Christians who remain alive. In either case, Christ will personally take care of those who *have* hope upon His return from heaven. This stands in contrast to the Greek philosophers, most of whom believe that there will be no resurrection from the dead (Acts 17:18, 20, 32).

> The excessive sorrow of the children of this world, when they lose a friend is not to be wondered at. They bury their bones in the grave. They part, for all that they know or believe, with such

> a friend forever. The wife, the son, the daughter, they consign to silence—to decay—to dust, not expecting to meet them again. They look forward to no glorious resurrection, when that body shall rise, and when they shall be reunited to part no more. It is no wonder that they weep—for who would not weep when he believes that he parts with his friends forever?
>
> It is only the hope of future blessedness that can mitigate this sorrow. Religion reveals a brighter world—a world where all the pious shall be reunited; where the bonds of love shall be made stronger than they were here; where they shall never be severed again. It is only this hope that can soothe the pains of grief at parting; only when we can look forward to a better world, and feel that we shall see them again—love them again—love them forever, that our tears are made dry.[54]

"For if we believe that Jesus died and rose again" (4:14)—another way of saying, "*Since* we believe *this*, then we can also believe what follows." The gospel of Christ—indeed, everything we call Christianity—rests upon the real and historical facts of Jesus' death, burial, and resurrection (1 Cor. 15:3–4). "Even so, God will bring with Him those … in Jesus"—it is necessary to leave these words in their context, particularly regarding the order of events described. Paul does *not* say, "Those who will be resurrected will also appear in the sky with Jesus," because this undermines the very purpose of the resurrection. Rather, there will be a grand reunion that God will orchestrate: Christ will appear in the clouds (Acts 1:9–11), and those who have died will be raised from the dead to join Him. The phrase ("will bring with Him") is thus explained in the following verses.

Yet, this also begs the question (among others): what is the state of being of those people *right now*? We do not have to answer this to understand or teach the present passage. Suffice it to say that they are "with the Lord" (as in 2 Cor. 5:8–9 or Phil. 1:23)—whatever that means, and whatever that necessarily involves, we are not certain; yet we know that such souls are well taken care of. "Those who have fallen asleep in Jesus" refers to those who have been faithful to Him until they died (Rev. 2:10).

54 Barnes, *Barnes' Notes* (electronic), on 4:13.

The Order of Events at the Second Coming (4:15–18): The question here is not *whether* Christ will appear, for this is certain (4:15). The "coming of the Lord" is not a figure of speech in this case but refers to a real and future event: "Christ … *will appear* a second time for salvation without reference to sin, to those who eagerly await Him" (Heb. 9:28, emphasis added). This is a given; Paul as well as the Thessalonians understand this.

What follows, however, is not Paul's opinion of what will happen but what God has revealed to him "by the word of the Lord." The date or timing of the event, and other details, he does not say, nor do we need to know.

What we *do* know is that at the time of Christ's appearance, "we who are alive" will not be raised before those who have died. It is appropriate that those who have had to taste of death will receive priority over those who have never had to die. Thus, there is a certain *order* or *sequence* to this great event. This also answers the question on the Thessalonians' minds, "What will become of those who have died in the Lord?"

"For the Lord Himself will descend from heaven with a shout" (4:16) —a passage that gives chills even to the most faithful believer. For now, Christ allows men to do what they want, say what they want, and ignore Him all they want. For now, Christ does not destroy those who blaspheme Him and mock His holy name. For now, it may appear that the world will go on forever just as it always has, that Christ's presence among men is an ancient holdover from a primitive and superstitious world, and that He has been replaced by skeptics, atheists, and hedonists. For now, mockers will come—indeed, they are everywhere around us, and there are far more of them than there are believers (2 Pet. 3:3–9).

But when Christ appears—not if, but *when*—this will all change, and it will never go back to how it is today. Christ will not appear secretly; quite the opposite, He will descend with a war cry of One who seeks to vindicate believers *and* bring divine retribution against unbelievers (see comments on 2 Thess. 1:6–9). He will manifest Himself as a Glorious

King who will reward His servants but destroy those who hate Him (Luke 19:11–27, in principle).

This "shout" [lit., commanding cry] reminds us of Christ's loud voice with which He summoned Lazarus from his grave (John 11:43). Jesus also said, "Do not marvel at this; for an hour is coming, in which all who are in the tombs will hear His voice, and will come forth" (John 5:28).[55] Paul does not address those who will be resurrected to stand trial, so to speak—i.e., those resurrected to judgment (John 5:29)—but only those who will be resurrected to gain their reward. This group of people is the only one with which he is presently concerned.

"The voice of {the} archangel" indicates more than merely a signal command but implies a "voice" of great approval. Beyond this, we can only speculate, since none of us has ever seen, much less heard, an archangel; frankly, we cannot even be certain what (or who) an "archangel" *is*. The "trumpet of God" alludes to the summoning of the camp of Israel in the wilderness with trumpets (Num. 10:1–10), the announcement of certain festivals (Lev. 23:24), or a call to war (Num. 31:6). More specifically, however, it alludes to the announcement of *God's presence among the people*, as what the Israelites heard at the foot of Mount Sinai (Exod. 19:16–18 and 20:18). When Jesus appears, there will be a loud, distinct, and unmistakable *announcement* of His presence, one that the entire world will hear—one that even the *dead* will hear.

"And the dead in Christ will rise first" (4:16)—the emphasis here is on the word "first," as in a matter of priority. These will not just "rise" from their graves, but they will rise to meet the Lord in the air, having been already resurrected from the dead. We have no reason to assume a "spiritual" or figurative resurrection here—i.e., one that does not involve an actual bodily resurrection from the grave. It is not important or necessary for us to know *how* God will raise the dead, but that He *can* and *will* raise them. Just as Jesus literal body was raised from the dead, so will the bodies of those who have died "in the Lord."

---

55 "The word *keleusma* means command, or order, a military command as in commanding horses or men; Christ will come issuing commands" (Curtis A. Cates, "Words of Comfort for Anxious Saints," *Studies*, 162).

How long will these resurrected people linger upon the earth before ascending into glory? Not long, it appears—but long enough (in my opinion) to substantiate before all unbelievers that *those who were raised were right to have believed in God.* In other words, one of the *purposes* of the resurrection is to vindicate the righteous before the eyes of the wicked and unbelieving.

"Then we who are alive" (4:17a)—i.e., in this order, according to this sequence. First the dead are raised from the grave *and* to meet Christ "in the clouds"; after this, the living believers will be raised to meet Christ and those resurrected "in the air."[56] This latter group will be "caught up"—the same language Paul used in describing his vision of Paradise (2 Cor. 12:2, 4; see also Acts 8:39 and Rev. 12:5).[57] The context of Paul's experience was a vision; what he speaks of here (in 4:17), however, is in a literal context. Believers will be raised to meet the Lord in the air; we have no reason to believe otherwise.

Paul does not speak here of a localized appearance (as in Christ's personal vengeance against Jerusalem—Mat. 24:27–31, Luke 21:20–

---

56 "'In clouds'—not simply because clouds suggested themselves as convenient vehicles for transportation through space but because clouds are a regular feature of biblical theophanies [lit., showings of God—MY WORDS]; the divine glory is veiled in clouds, shines forth from them and retreats into them. … Specifically relevant to the NT background are the 'clouds of heaven' with which 'one like a son of man' came to be presented before the Ancient of Days in Dan 7:13…" (Bruce, *WBC*, 102).

57 "Caught up" comes from *harpazo*, "to seize, catch up, snatch away" (Strong, *Dictionary* [electronic], G726). Some call this a "rapture" (from the Latin [Vulgate], *rapere*) which is accurate in a limited sense; but this cannot be confused with what Premillennialists call "*the* Rapture." In this latter case, the church—both the living and the dead— will allegedly be "raptured" from the earth while the rest of the world slogs through a seven-year-long Tribulation, culminating in an apocalyptic battle called Armageddon. When people try to reconcile Paul's words with their fanciful "interpretations" of Dan. 9, Mat. 24, and *Revelation*, they run into serious and irreconcilable problems. This is not because the passages are in error or confusing; rather, they are being taken out of context, misapplied, and forced to fit a pre-determined agenda (i.e., Premillennialism, or the doctrine of the [coming] thousand-year reign of Christ on earth). "It is ironic that 1 Thessalonians 4 is the chief proof text of a theory that says Christ will return secretly and invisibly, given that this is one of the 'noisiest' passages in the New Testament" (Shane Scott, "Not Grieve as Others," *A Life Worthy*, 230).

22, etc.); he certainly does not speak of a "spiritual" or "symbolic" appearance that has already happened. Rather, he speaks of a universal event: *everyone* who has died in the Lord will be raised; *everyone* who still lives by faith will be caught up to Him. Jesus said, "I am the resurrection and the life; he who believes in Me will live even if he dies, and everyone who lives and believes in Me will never die" (John 11:23–26). This speaks of the future resurrection of all those who believe in Him: those who die "will live"; those who live "will never die." This corresponds exactly with what Paul explains to the Thessalonians.

Paul has also said elsewhere, "Behold, I tell you a mystery; we will not all sleep, but we will all be changed, in a moment, in the twinkling of an eye, at the last trumpet; for the trumpet will sound, and the dead will be raised imperishable, and we [who have *not* died—MY WORDS] will be changed" (1 Cor. 15:51–52). This is consistent with the present passage: not everyone will die, but *all* will be raised to be with Christ. In the process of being raised, "we will be changed"—i.e., we will receive a spiritual body that conforms to our spiritual existence. This earthly "tent" conforms to this life and this world; but "we have a building [body] from God, a house not made with hands, eternal in the heavens" (2 Cor. 5:1–4). This is because "flesh and blood cannot inherit the kingdom of God" (1 Cor. 15:50): we will not enter glory with this earthly body.

"And so we shall always be with the Lord" (4:17b). This is the final reward for faithful believers: they will be with the One whom they have loved, honored, and worshiped, and for whom they sacrificed everything here on earth. Paul later wrote, "I have fought the good fight, I have finished the course, I have kept the faith; in the future there is laid up for me the crown of righteousness, which the Lord, the righteous Judge, will award to me on that day; and not only to me, but also to all who have loved His appearing" (2 Tim. 4:7–8).[58] Those who believe in the first appearance of Jesus, "bringing salvation to all men" (Titus 2:11)—and who live accordingly—will join Him when He appears a second time to bring them home (Heb. 9:28).

58 "Love His appearing" in 2 Tim. 4:8 refers to Jesus' incarnate (human) existence; it is not a reference to any "appearing" after that.

Again, Paul does not mention here the resurrection of those who died *outside* the Lord, those for whom there is "no hope" of salvation. He does believe that they, too, will be resurrected: "there shall certainly be a resurrection of both the righteous and the wicked" (Acts 24:15). This is consistent with what Jesus taught: "Do not marvel at this; for an hour is coming, in which all who are in the tombs will hear His voice, and will come forth; those who did the good deeds to a resurrection of life, those who committed the evil deeds to a resurrection of judgment" (John 5:28–29).

After the resurrection of the righteous and after the faithful are caught up to be with Him in the air, Christ will exact His divine vengeance upon the wicked world that refused to believe in Him. The rest of the dead will be resurrected—not to join the company of the saints, but to face their sentencing before the Judge. Those who remain on earth will likely perish in the fiery judgment that engulfs the earth, just as the inhabitants of Sodom and Gomorrah perished in their own fiery execution (Gen. 19:24–25, 2 Thess. 1:6–9).

In any case, we have no reason to believe that the world will continue to exist "just as it was from the beginning of creation" (2 Pet. 3:4), but that Christ will most certainly destroy it. It is the righteous that are staving off God's wrath against all unrighteousness (Rom. 1:18); once they are removed—once the "light" and "salt" no longer provide any illumination or preservation (Mat. 5:13–16)—there is no reason to delay divine judgment any longer. God will call all humankind to stand before Him and His Son; "For we must all appear before the judgment seat of Christ, so that each one may be recompensed for his deeds in the body, according to what he has done, whether good or bad" (2 Cor. 5:10). We will revisit this scene of destruction, however, in 2 *Thessalonians*.

"Therefore comfort one another with these words" (4:18). These words offer *no* comfort to those who are faithless or disobedient; however, they describe scenes of inexpressible joy for those who are faithful and obedient.

> God's enemies and the persecutors of Christians are clearly doomed. They don't expect what is coming, but it will come.

> When they aren't looking and when they think that all is well, the judgment of God will overtake them and there will be no escape. Most Christians readily accept this to be true, but where is the comfort? For many, the notion of finding comfort in others being judged is positively unchristian. However, the Scriptures reveal multiple reasons why judgment is both comfort and relief. First, judgment means that the persecution will come to an end. Persecutors, even at their worst, are limited. Eventually we escape their grip. They can seize our belongings, harms our bodies, and take our lives, but after that, they are powerless. One way or another, we will gain relief from their persecution. Second, the certainty of judgment means that those who have done heinous things against God and His saints will get what they deserve. The punishment is not excessive. It is just. God's judgment is righteous.[59]

An incredible and breathtaking reward awaits those "in Christ"—whether they are living or dead. This creates a powerful incentive to continue in obedience to Christ regardless of the sufferings that one must face, since "the sufferings of this present time are not worthy to be compared with the glory that is to be revealed to us" (Rom. 8:18). Thus, the believer has a genuine and infallible *hope* that the rest of the world does not have, and God will most certainly fulfill this hope. As certain as Christ has raised from the dead and ascended into heaven, so He will return to gather His elect together at some future time. This ought to be a message upon which the church on earth often reflects.

Anticipation for Christ's Return (1 Thess. 5:1–11)

The Day of the Lord (5:1–3): The Thessalonians—not unlike people today—eagerly want to know the specifics of Christ's return. When the letter was read aloud to the congregation, you can almost hear someone in the group asking, "Yes, but *when* . . . ?" To this, Paul answers, "Now as to the time and the epochs, brethren,

59 Jared Hagan, "Relief to You Who Are Afflicted," *A Life Worthy*, 217–218.

you have no need of anything to be written to you" (5:1). This situation is remarkably similar to the apostles' question to Jesus just prior to His ascension *to* heaven: "Lord, is it at this time You are restoring the kingdom to Israel?" And Jesus replied, "It is not for you to know times or epochs which the Father has fixed by His own authority" (Acts 1:6–7). "Time" refers to an indefinite period *of* time, or to a fixed point of reference *in* time. "Epoch" refers to a *right* time, as an optimum occasion for something to happen; or the season in which such opportunity is to happen.[60]

"You have no need" (5:1) can be taken one of two ways: **first**, you do not need to know this information (to fulfill your commitment to God); **second**, if you are always ready for His coming, it really does not matter *when* He comes. In this text, both meanings seem to apply equally. Paul had already told them that they could not know the hour of His coming (5:2); but the Master's servants should always be ready for His return (Luke 12:35–40, in principle).

"For you yourselves know" (5:2)—obviously, Paul has already taught what follows. "Like a thief in the night" refers to the *suddenness* of Christ's return. It is an expression that Jesus used with reference to His judgment against Jerusalem (Mat. 24:42–44) and His judgment against any of the impenitent churches of Asia (Rev. 3:3, 16:16). Peter uses the same expression about Christ's Second Coming (2 Peter 3:10). Thus, "the day of the Lord *will come*" (emphasis added), but the exact *time* of His coming will catch off guard all those who are unprepared for it (as in Luke 17:26–30).[61]

The "day of the Lord" expression has different applications in the NT. In Mat. 24:42, it refers to Christ's judgment against Jerusalem (in AD 70); in Acts 2:20, it refers to the great upheaval to the Jewish system caused by the establishment of His church (AD 30). Here (in 5:2), "the

60 Thayer, *Lexicon* (electronic), G5550 and G2540, respectively.

61 I understand Jesus' words (in Luke 17:22ff) to describe His judgment against Jerusalem and the Jewish nation, not the end of the world. Nonetheless, the principles remain the same: in both cases, those who refuse to prepare for this day of judgment will be completely surprised by it.

day of the Lord" is directly associated with the day of Christ's Second Coming (as in 2 Thess. 2:1–2). We cannot assume that the same words or phrases have the same application if indeed the context changes. It is context that determines the ultimate use and meaning of words, not just the definition of individual words or phrases by themselves. Common features to all uses of "the day of the Lord" include:

- They all refer to a "day" or time that God has fixed by His own authority.
- When these "days" will happen cannot be known precisely until they occur in history, but neither can men prevent, postpone, change, or avoid these "days" once they have been decreed.
- While these "days" cannot be known precisely, God nonetheless warns men that they are coming so that they can be prepared for them (through repentance and righteous living). Such warnings are invariably and divinely revealed through prophecy but are also accompanied by signs or harbingers that ought to have been taken seriously (as in Amos 4:6–12).
- They are all divinely appointed events imposed upon humankind because of sin—whether due to impenitence or as a means of atoning for sin. In this sense, they are *always* a "day" of judgment, although what serves as judgment to some will be salvation to others. (In God's judgment against ancient Israel, for example, He punished the entire nation for its infidelity to His covenant, yet in the very same process He purified that nation for its future participation in the salvation of the entire world.)
- They all create a great upheaval, major transition, or termination of something—society, nation, religion, means of salvation (covenant), or realm of man in general. In one context or another, it depicts a turning point (of some kind) after which the realm or people affected will *never be the same.*
- While "the day of the Lord" certainly has a negative aspect to it (as divine judgment against sin), its ultimate purpose is to advance God's will in heaven and/or the earth. Dealing with sin (or, removing impenitent sinners from the realm of men) provides an occasion and opportunity for the living to turn to God for salvation

> rather than remain in their condemned state of being. Even in the *final* "day of the Lord," the destruction of the world provides for the eternal union of Christ and His church in the hereafter. This brings about what God has always desired through the creation of man: "I will be their God, and they will be My people" (2 Cor. 6:16, etc.).

"Peace and safety" (5:3) imitates the words of the deceitful prophets who convinced Judah not to worry about Babylon and thus led many Jews into a false sense of security (Jer. 6:14, 8:11, 23:17, Ezek. 13:10, and 16). Those people refused to listen to God's warnings of judgment and chose instead to receive the smooth and flattering words of impostors. As it was then, so it will be just before the End: men will be proclaiming "Peace!" to the world, even as the Lord prepares to destroy it. Such delusion will be the result of a mass rejection of God and their reliance instead upon human effort to "save" the world from its own demise. "Like labor pains" is another analogy of the suddenness of this event: you can know that it is coming, but you cannot predict exactly when.

"And they will not escape"—"they" referring to those caught unaware by and unprepared for the suddenness of Christ's return. This indicates that His Second Coming will be salvation to those who believe but judgment to the disobedient and disbelieving (1 Cor. 1:18, 2 Cor. 2:15–16). Those who claim that Jesus has already returned "invisibly" or "secretly" overlook this most important detail. When He comes, it will be obvious to all, for *destruction* will come upon all who have resisted Him, while those who have believed in Him will come forth from their graves. This will be an event that simply cannot be ignored, misinterpreted, or mistaken for something else. "Some of the Thessalonians were very concerned about the destiny of dead Christians [cf. 4:13]; but, after disposing of that problem, showing that death cannot make the slightest difference in eternal rewards, Paul then thundered the warning that when the Second Advent does occur, vast numbers of earth's population shall be totally unprepared for it, and that even Christians should exercise the utmost diligence to be prepared for Jesus' coming."[62]

---

62 Coffman, *Commentary*, 59–60; bracketed words are mine.

The "Sons of Day" Will Be Ready (5:4–7): In sharp contrast to those who are completely surprised and unprepared for Christ's return, Christians will be anticipating this and completely prepared for it (5:4). "Darkness" here refers to spiritual ignorance or darkness of understanding (in this case, of this information). By implication, it is a *chosen* darkness since Christ has come to be the "Light of the world" (John 8:12) and His resurrection was meant to be believed (Acts 17:30–31). In other words, there is no excuse for such darkness or ignorance, yet many will embrace it all the same. Faithful Christians will be the *only* people in the entire world who will be genuinely prepared for Christ's return, *regardless* of when He comes. In fact, *when* He comes is entirely irrelevant to them: they will be ready whenever it happens.

"For you are all sons of light and sons of day" (5:5)—i.e., you who have been enlightened by Christ's gospel have no reason to live in spiritual ignorance or moral darkness (Eph. 5:6–10). This spiritual illumination ought to produce a state of readiness and expectancy rather than one of confusion or unpreparedness (cf. Luke 12:35–44). "Let us not sleep as others do" (5:6)—while "sleep" can refer to the state of being dead (as in 4:13), here it obviously has a different meaning since the context has changed. He cannot mean, "Let us not be physically dead like the others" because this makes no sense. Here, Paul uses "sleep" as a state of delusion, numbness, and moral inattention. "The others" refers to partakers of (moral) darkness, as he mentions in the next verse.

"For those who sleep … those who get drunk" (5:7)—i.e., those who engage in worldly behavior choose to do so under the cover of darkness; this is a literal statement.[63] While Paul's comments here most certainly apply to those who resist the gospel altogether (see John 3:18–21), the context serves also as a warning to *Christians* who are being inattentive or indifferent toward their moral responsibilities. In any case, Paul means: "Do not act like those who live in the darkness; you Christians, of all people, should know better than this."

---

63 "The language here is not figurative but factual: night is the time when people sleep; night is the time when people get drunk (and therefore reckless)" (Bruce, *WBC*, 112).

Putting on God's Armor (5:8–11): "But since we are of the day" (5:8)—i.e., since we belong to Christ completely, "let us lay aside the deeds of darkness and put on the armor of light" (Rom. 13:12). The word "sober" here literally means serious-minded, self-controlled, and (by implication) attentive in carrying out one's charge. Paul then uses metaphors from the "full armor of God" in Eph. 6:10–17. (Paul wrote *First Thessalonians* years before *Ephesians*, so he develops the "armor" metaphor in that letter than here.)

The military allusions that Paul uses here are appropriate since Christians are indeed engaged in a spiritual battle "against the world forces of this darkness and the spiritual forces of wickedness" (Eph. 6:12). The "breastplate of faith and love" alludes to the chest protection that a Roman soldier would wear into battle. This protects his vital organs, and especially his heart, which the ancients believed was the center of one's emotions. The "helmet," however, protects the head—the center of a man's rational thoughts. The believer's hope in God is not an emotional thing, but rests upon evidence, information, and divine promises. In effect, Paul says "You need to protect your *head* and your *heart* to engage your Christian ministry." These figures of speech, drawn from the military, imply a spiritual battle in which the believer confronts (and fights against) the forces of this world.[64]

God is against the ungodly world, but He offers divine help and protection for those who are faithful "in Christ." Thus, "God has not destined us for wrath" (5:9)—and yet, this "wrath" is a very real expression of His divine indignation toward all unrighteousness (Rom. 1:18). When we talk about salvation, "the wrath of God" is what we are being saved *from* (John 3:36, Rom. 5:9). Sinners will personally *experience* this wrath if they do not come to their senses, repent of their sin, and enter a covenant relationship with God.

Thus, those "destined" for wrath are simply those who have rejected salvation; their destiny is determined by (or the result of) their own decision, not God. The satanic, self-serving, and God-hating world is

64 For much more detail on this subject, I recommend my *Galatians and Ephesians Commentary* (Spiritbuilding Publishers); go to www.spiritbuilding.com/chad.

"destined" for wrath, while the bride of Christ (His church) is destined for salvation (Rom. 8:29–30, Eph. 1:3–7, etc.). This salvation is not through the Christian's own good deeds, but "through our Lord Jesus Christ"—i.e., what He accomplished: His virtue, His worthiness, His power, etc. "Obtain" here is used in a passive sense, as in one's reception of something, rather than one's having gained it through his own effort.[65] On the other hand, this salvation requires one's personal faith *in* Jesus Christ (1 Pet. 1:9), which demands an allegiance to Him above all else.

Christ died *for* us (5:10), because our own death would not obtain anything on its own; in fact, nothing we do can compare with or duplicate what He has done.[66] If we respond appropriately to His death, then "whether we are awake or asleep"—in a play on the "sleep" idea, Paul returns to the figurative use of sleep, meaning one's state of death—"we will live together with Him." This picks up where he left off in 4:13–18, where Christ will gather those who have died in Him as well as those who are still alive when He returns in the clouds.[67] This concurs with John's words: "The world is passing away, and also its lusts; but the one who does the will of God lives forever" (1 John 2:17).

> As Paul brings this discussion of the second coming to a close, he stresses that the *parousia* is not simply about an event, but about a person. "Whether we are awake or asleep we might live *with him*" (vs. 10). Just as the significance of a wedding is about the relationship of the wedded rather than the date of the event, the hope of the second coming is centered on the one who is coming, the Lord Jesus. This prospect, eternal union in Christ, should encourage and fortify us, just as the hope of the resurrection does (cf. 4:18).[68]

---

65 Adapted from JFB, *Commentary* (electronic), on 5:9.

66 "This statement, then, that 'Christ died for us, in order that we might live with him,' is the most explicit statement in the Thessalonian letters of the saving purpose of the death of Christ" (Bruce, *WBC*, 114).

67 Romans 14:7–9 is applicable here: "For not one of us lives for himself, and not one dies for himself; for if we live, we live for the Lord, or if we die, we die for the Lord; therefore whether we live or die, we are the Lord's. For to this end Christ died and lived again, that He might be Lord both of the dead and of the living."

68 Scott, "Not Grieve as Others," *A Life Worthy*, 233.

"Therefore, encourage … and build up" (5:11)—similar to what he wrote in 4:18. "Encourage" literally means "to give comfort (or, impart courage) to" someone; "build up" literally refers to the building of a house, and (by application) "to edify, strengthen, or promote growth."[69] "The apostle has advanced no fewer than six criteria for achieving adequate and effective preparation in anticipation of the Lord's return: (1) don't sleep (5:6); (2) watch (5:6); (3) be sober (5:6, 8); (4) put on Christian armor (5:8); (5) exhort each other (5:11); and (6) edify one another (5:11). If we Christians will place these elements into effect in our lives, we will have done much to prepare ourselves for the Second Coming."[70]

Practical Conduct and Final Remarks (1 Thess. 5:12–28)

What Is Expected of Believers (5:12–22): Having exhorted the Christians at Thessalonica to be "sons of day" rather than imitate those who live in moral darkness, Paul now offers practical considerations for this lifestyle. In other words, living in the light is not a mere status to which one attains, nor is it merely a good idea. It must be accompanied by conduct that agrees with one's profession of faith.

First, Paul instructs these Christians to "appreciate" (or know the value of) the elders whom they have appointed to shepherd them (5:12–13). The description of these men can refer *particularly* to elders, as will be discussed. At the same time, we are to appreciate *all* laborers in the church, whoever they might be (see 1 Cor. 16:15–18). In this present text, these men are those who:

- ❑ **"diligently labor over you":** Elder work involves actual *work* ("labor"). It is not merely a position to fill or a status to enjoy; it is a ministry to which a man devotes himself and promises to fulfill with all his endeavor. "Diligence" does not only refer to effort that is earnest but also effective and efficient; it is an intelligent application of energy (as in Rom. 12:11 and 2 Peter 1:5).

69 Thayer, *Lexicon* (electronic), G3870 and 3618, respectively.

70 Dave Miller, "Preparing for the 'Day of the Lord,'" *Studies*, 182).

- **"have charge over you in the Lord":** This cannot refer to Christians generally or to ministers of the word. It refers exclusively to appointed elders who shepherd their flock and have a "charge" over those who appointed them (1 Peter 5:1–3). This "charge" is to oversee the spiritual welfare of the congregation; promote sound doctrine as well as defend against false teaching (Titus 1:9); and serve as examples to those whom they oversee. For this reason, Christians are to "Obey your leaders and submit to them, for they keep watch over your souls as those who will give an account. Let them do this with joy and not with grief, for this would be unprofitable for you" (Heb. 13:17). This does not mean that elders will assume responsibility for those under their charge; it means that they will answer to God for how *they* (the elders) managed their own responsibility toward those who appointed them.
- **"give you instruction":** This is not just good advice (although this, too) but teaching from God's word. Elders have a moral responsibility to instruct and admonish those members whom they shepherd; these members have a moral responsibility to receive this instruction, respond to this admonition, and follow these men's godly examples. "Remember those who led you, who spoke the word of God to you; and considering the result of their conduct, imitate their faith" (Heb. 13:7).

"And that you esteem them very highly in love because of their work" (5:13)—i.e., not just give elders a token nod of acknowledgment, but treat them with great honor and gratitude. Ideally, such men have devoted their lives to those whom they oversee, and this is worthy of the congregation's deep respect. By implication, it also means to take care of these men (financially and otherwise): "The elders who rule well are to be considered worthy of double honor [i.e., remuneration—MY WORD], especially those who work hard at preaching and teaching" (1 Tim. 5:17).

"Love" provides the right context and motive for this respect. In other words, one should not give esteem to such men simply because that person wishes to gain personal advantage with them, but because it is the right thing to do in the sight of God. "Live in peace with one another"—likely, this is a reference to all those who labor within the church, as opposed to rivalry, jealousy, or strife (see Gal. 5:13–14).

Paul then urges the Thessalonians to support others in the group besides its spiritual leaders—in this case, those who are less mature, less experienced, or who are struggling (5:14).

- **"admonish the unruly":** "Admonish" means, in essence, to remind one of that to which he or she originally committed. It is an encouragement to do well, and at the same time a warning against neglect or giving up. The "unruly" (or, undisciplined; disorderly) can have reference to all kinds of misbehaviors; it refers to anything that is inappropriate, insubordinate (as a soldier to his commanding officer), or deviating from an expected behavior.[71]
- **"encourage the fainthearted":** In essence, this means to give moral support, consolation, and reassurance to those who are spiritually struggling, or regarding whatever affects their spiritual outlook. Paul does not want believers to lose heart (Gal. 6:9; see Heb. 12:3). It often takes the encouragement of fellow believers—those who can *give* such support—to get through times of discouragement, feelings of inadequacy, or seemingly overwhelming circumstances.[72]
- **"help the weak":** This is a broad directive with numerous practical applications. The "weak" can be many different people and for varied reasons. Often, however, it boils down to this: they are those whose faith simply is not (yet) as strong or grounded as it needs to be, thus they grapple with Christian responsibilities. Thus, "we who are strong ought to bear the weaknesses of those without strength and not just please ourselves" (Rom. 15:1).
  - "Weak" in this context does not refer to the unwilling, as those who are rebelling against the Lord's commands; Scripture never teaches us to enable resistance or irresponsibility in any form. Rather, it refers to those who do not yet have the knowledge, spiritual maturity, or experience to deal with the rigors of discipleship.

---

71 Thayer, *Lexicon* (electronic), G813.

72 "Fainthearted" is from *oligopsuchous*—lit., "little-souled." "Local conditions often cause some to lose heart and wish to drop out, be quitters. These must be held in line" (Robertson, *Word Pictures*, 37).

- How do we help the weak? This can be as simple as offering an encouraging word, or as involved as taking someone into your care for a season until he (or she) is able to take care of himself. It may involve spiritual counseling or financial support; it may require an hour of your time or a prolonged commitment. Whatever it takes is appropriate, if that person is sincere in his willingness to grow and produces visible and measurable results from your efforts over time.

❑ **"be patient with everyone":** This is another general directive that has broad applications and implications. "Patience" is the withholding (or delaying) of condemnation or punishment toward a person in anticipation of his reform. It is something that God shows to us for this very same reason (Rom. 2:4, 1 Tim. 1:16, 2 Pet. 3:9, etc.). Patience is a virtue of godly love (1 Cor. 13:4) and a "fruit of the Spirit" (Gal. 5:22). It is related to tolerance and forbearance—things that are necessary in dealing with the imperfections of others in their less-than-perfect treatment of us (Col. 3:12–13). The phrase "with everyone" certainly refers to those within the church but can apply also to those who have yet to obey the Lord. Christians should be patient in their teaching and prayers for such people, in hopes that they will "come to their senses and escape through the snare of the devil" (2 Tim. 2:24–26). Thus, "mutual discipline must be exercised by all the members. It is wrong to leave all this to pastors [elders]."[73]

"See to it that no one repays another with evil for evil" (5:15), because Christians must not be a people of vengeance, spite, or retaliation. (This goes for Christians toward their *spouses* as well as others.) God is the Avenger of all wrongs, and we cannot assume His role by taking such matters into our own hands (Rom. 12:17–20, 1 Pet. 3:8–9). We are supposed to pray for our enemies (Mat. 5:44), not seek their harm or ruin—no matter what they have done to us. If Christ could entrust His Father with carrying out the justice that was due Him (Christ), then so can we (1 Pet. 2:23). No doubt Paul's words here serve as a warning against those who might be embittered against unbelievers in

73 Hendriksen, *NTC*, 136; bracketed word is mine.

Thessalonica who had caused them so much grief (recall 2:14). "Seek after that which is good"—i.e., practice godly love toward all people. This means to seek their best interest *regardless* of what they do or do not do. This is what God does, and we are to be imitators of Him (Eph. 5:1).

For the next several verses (5:16–22), Paul gives a series of brief but potent directives intended for all Christians to obey:

- ❑ **"Rejoice always"** (5:16)—not only when things go as we had hoped, but even when our circumstances are uncomfortable and seem unfavorable. Joy is supposed to be one of the hallmarks of believers and a "fruit" of the Spirit (Gal. 5:22). Since we have a priceless inheritance awaiting us in the hereafter, we ought to live accordingly! Thus, even amid trials, distresses, and persecutions, we still have good reason to rejoice in the fact that we have fellowship with our Creator (Phil. 4:4, 1 Pet. 1:3–9).
- ❑ **"Pray without ceasing"** (5:17) seems a perfect accompaniment to rejoicing always. One who does not pray has no legitimate reason for rejoicing; one who rejoices can only do so because he has prayerful communion with his Father. "Without ceasing" does not mean "at every moment," but as a regular habit. Prayer should be as rhythmic a behavior to the believer as breathing is to the human body.
- ❑ **"In everything give thanks"** (5:18), because Christians should be a grateful, thankful people—not only for prayers that were answered as we had hoped, but also for those which were answered differently than we had hoped (Phil. 4:6). In fact, we should be thankful that God does not always give us everything we ask for, since we ask from a finite, imperfect, and often selfish perspective. It is God's will that we be "overflowing with gratitude" (Col. 2:7) since gratitude and reverence go hand in hand. It is "God's will" that we be prayerful and always grateful in our prayers.
- ❑ **"Do not quench the Spirit"** (5:19) likely has reference to miraculous manifestations of the Spirit, in the form of so-call spiritual gifts.[74] To "quench" means to extinguish (as a fire), stifle,

74 I have an entire chapter devoted to this very thought in my book, *The Holy Spirit of God: A Biblical Perspective* (Waynesville, OH: Spiritbuilding Publishers, 2010); go to www.spiritbuilding.com/chad.

or suppress.[75] The warning here is to those who undervalue or dismiss altogether some of the miraculous abilities of other believers endowed with the Spirit. Not only do these first people fail to benefit from what is offered, but they also prevent others from benefiting; furthermore, they stand in the way of the reason *for* such gifts, which were designed by the Spirit to edify the church and support its "common good" (1 Cor. 12:7).

- ❑ **"Do not despise prophetic utterances [or, prophecy]"** (5:20) restates the same idea, but with emphasis on the prophetic nature of these gifts. It is entirely wrong for someone to hold in contempt a message given to the church by direct inspiration of the Holy Spirit. To "prophesy" in the formal sense does not necessarily mean to predict the future (although it can mean this as well, as in Acts 21:10–11). It can also mean to proclaim God's truth—specifically, by inspiration of the Spirit—or provide any inspired teaching or direction on a given matter. There is no reason to believe that the Thessalonians are in fact quenching the Spirit or despising prophetic utterances; yet there is nothing to say that some are *not*, either. Regardless, Paul gives a strong warning not to let it happen (or to put an immediate stop to it if it *is* happening).
- ❑ **"But examine everything carefully"** (5:21–22)—to "examine" implies testing something (against an approved standard) to determine its fitness or value. Also, do not accept anything too hastily or without a proper discernment of its true value (Rom. 12:9). Instead of suppressing the message of the Spirit to the church or holding His prophets in contempt, Paul instructs the Thessalonians to be wise in their examination of all things (5:21a).

This instruction applies to the situation at hand: if the Thessalonian Christians are being confronted with both genuine and false prophets, they need to investigate the matter wisely and judiciously. But the application of Paul's instruction ("Examine everything carefully, etc.") goes well beyond the Thessalonians' immediate context. *All* Christians are to be wise and discerning in their estimation of what they accept as truth, what they practice in their lives, and their general conduct

75 Thayer, *Lexicon* (electronic), G4570.

as representatives of Christ. Paul's words serve as a brief yet excellent method by which to evaluate everything that will confront Christians.

- ❑ **"Hold fast to that which is good"** (5:21b) is a general descriptor that applies to *anything* that comes from God—teaching, blessings, lessons learned, people, etc. If it *is* good, then we would be foolish to ignore or reject it. On the other hand, whatever is evil—even if it bears the *appearance* of evil—then we are to stay clear of it. To "abstain … evil" (5:22) is also a general descriptor, but because of this it is all-encompassing. Paul did not have to itemize everything that is evil, thus giving us permission to engage in anything that is not on the "list." (Such is the reasoning of some: "Paul didn't say I *couldn't* do this!") If the teaching, thing, or practice is inconsistent with God's holy nature, then it is *evil,* having come from this world rather than given to us "from above" (see James 1:17 and 3:13–18). Lenski adds: "The worst forms of wickedness consist in perversions of the truth, of spiritual lies, although today many look upon these forms with indifference and regard them [as being] rather harmless."[76]

Final Admonitions (5:23–28): "Now may the God of peace Himself sanctify you entirely" (5:23). God does not want only a part of the believer sanctified, but the *whole* of him; likewise, each believer cannot be only half-sanctified (and thus remain half-corrupted) but must be *wholly* sanctified. "Sanctify" means "to make holy; to consecrate; to cleanse by expiation or atonement"[77] (recall comments on 4:3ff). To have fellowship with us, God must possess us completely (1 Cor. 6:19–20); but to possess us completely, we must be wholly or completely prepared for our presentation before Him—"holy and blameless and beyond approach" (Col. 1:21–22).

This means that the entirety of our existence—spirit, soul, and body—must be properly cleansed and prepared for this very purpose. The "God of peace" cannot allow disunity or disharmony of those who minister

76 Lenski, *Interpretation*, 363; bracketed words are mine.

77 Thayer, *Lexicon* (electronic), G37.

to Him; "peace" necessarily implies unity, completion, and the absence of conflict. "At the coming of our Lord Jesus Christ" provides the future context for Paul's words. He says, "When Christ returns, God will bring you to the *fullest expression* of what it means to be 'human'—like Christ was on earth, so you shall be perfected in every sense."

This begs the question: what does Paul mean by "spirit, soul, and body"? It is unlikely that any answer to this will satisfy every person's inquiry into this most intriguing subject.[78] Even so, I will attempt here to provide at least an intelligent response.

- ❑ "Spirit" is from the Greek *pneuma,* which is translated "soul," "spirit," "Spirit," "spiritual," "breath," or "wind" in the NT, depending upon context. The explanations for this word are long and complex, both in classical Greek and in Christian theology. To summarize, it may be said: one's *spirit* is that non-tangible, invisible part of his actual existence that animates his physical body upon this earth. Thus, every person is both physical and spiritual: he has a physical body, and he has a spirit that occupies or uses that body for that person to be "alive" in an earthly sense. (Some have said—rightly, I believe—that we are all spiritual beings having a bodily experience on earth, rather than being physical bodies with a spiritual existence.) The severance of the spirit from the body is what we know as "death" (James 2:26); the reuniting of one's spirit with his physical body is what we know as "resurrection." This is the use of "spirit" in the context of Paul's words in our present text (5:23).
- ❑ "Soul" is from the Greek *psuche,* from which we get our English word "psyche" and "psychology." It has a related but different meaning from *pneuma. Psuche* also indicates a non-tangible and invisible aspect of our human existence, but it is not truly a separate entity

78 Hendriksen, for one, provides several different arguments in his five-page-long footnote (*NTC,* 146–150). His main argument is that Paul was not a "trichotomist," one who separates man's nature into three different parts. Yet, despite all his technical analysis, man really *does* have three different aspects to his human nature; this cannot be denied. In his opinion, "soul" and "spirit" speak of one and the same thing, and "body" is added after the fact; but this conclusion cannot be mandated by the biblical text. The fact that Paul—not us—separates "soul" from "spirit" is significant; there is no reason to think that he is simply restating himself.

from either one's physical body or his spiritual being. (We often *use* it this way—as in, "God can save your soul!"—but technically it is differentiated from "spirit." It is true, also, that the NT writers, when speaking of one's spiritual life rather than his physical life, will use "spirit" and "soul" interchangeably if both words are not in the same passage. Paul's use of both words in the same sentence is rare in Scripture, forcing us to see them as distinctly different ideas.)

"Soul" in this context refers to a person's mind, conscious thought, or rational existence. It is his awareness both of himself as a physical creature that engages the physical world *and* a spiritual being who can interact with (but not visibly see or enter) the spiritual realm. He can know about God, pray to Him, and imagine the heavenly world, but he remains fixed in this world until his *spirit*—not (technically) his soul—is released from his physical body. At the point of his death, his earthly consciousness ceases to exist; his thoughts or consciousness is limited to the spiritual realm. (This is what we generally believe to be true, anyway. We have no reason to believe that those who have died retain full consciousness of what continues to happen in this life after their death.)

The fact is: your *mind* can conceive of heaven, but it is limited to an earthly context; your *spirit* animates your earthly body, but it is more closely connected with God's world than this world. Physical death disconnects the *mind* from the earthly realm, blinding us to what is happening here. God has given your spirit factual *evidence* of the spiritual realm, but you only know about it through *faith* experienced in this earthly life; it is blinded to so much of its actual context. Thus, upon death, the human mind is blinded, while the spirit suddenly sees. Upon one's resurrection *from* the dead, however, it seems that neither the mind *nor* the spirit will be blind, but both will "see" with equal clarity. (There is no way I can prove any of this with absolute certainty; yet I have deducted it from all NT passages on this subject.)

- "Body" [Greek, *soma*] is the clearest of terms here. This refers to one's physical body (his "flesh") that serves as an earthly vehicle for

> his life here in the physical realm. There is nothing spiritual about the body itself; it is entirely biological or physiological. However, neither can the body be *alive* apart from its union with one's spiritual being. So then, there *is* something spiritual about every living *person,* but not his literal *body*.

What makes a person whole or complete is the union of his spirit (his otherworldly, invisible being), soul (his conscious awareness of both this world and the next), and body (his fleshly presence in this life). All fanciful theories of ghosts and zombies aside, we have no knowledge of a living body devoid of a spirit, a consciousness devoid of a body, or a spirit in God's realm that retains a consciousness of this human realm. This brings us back to the question: what does Paul mean by God preserving to completion our spirit, soul, and body? In our present, living state of being, we understand that our will (involving our spirit, mind, and physical body) is to surrender to God's will. But what of those who have already died in the Lord and no longer have a physical body or an earthly consciousness? Or does Paul even speak of these?

It is my understanding that Paul speaks here in a dual sense: ideally, with reference to a Christian's present state; and literally, in the resurrection (recall 4:13–17). Presently, we are to keep our spiritual life, thoughts, and physical body for the Lord. Since we are His possession, He must therefore have controlling interest over all three aspects of our existence. God also does His part in preserving us for our presentation with Him: He does everything we are unable to do, including forgiving us of our sins and consecrating us for service.

But Paul's words here (in 5:23) can only be truly fulfilled in the resurrection. At that time, the human spirit will reunite with its resurrected and glorified body (1 Cor. 15:42–44). That body will be seen by others, it will be tangible, and it will bear the identity of the person whose it was while he (or she) was on earth. However, it will be glorified in the same way Jesus' body was glorified when He appeared to His disciples after His death. At that time, the person whose spirit has reunited to his risen body will also have a conscious awareness of what is happening *to* him and *around* him.

It is this resurrected state of being that (I believe) Paul refers to when he says that the believer will be "preserved complete" by God's power. He is definite as to the context: "at the coming of our Lord Jesus Christ." Thus, the time and occasion of this preservation and completeness is specific, not general. Our ultimate completion—not in faith but in fact—will be when all believers appear before God as the bride of Christ, rendered blameless through the blood of Christ (Eph. 5:27). Such language cannot be fulfilled in our present condition (except as a promise that is contingent upon our continued faith) but speaks to a future-perfect context that we have not yet seen and in which we have not yet participated.

After he has been raised, the believer will then be caught up to heaven—in the same way Jesus ascended from the earth into the clouds—and he will be transformed into the glory commensurate with the Lord's (1 Cor. 15:50–53). As John wrote, "Beloved, now we are children of God, and it has not appeared as yet what we will be. We know that when He appears, we will be like Him, because we will see Him just as He is" (1 John 3:2). Christ will change our earthly body into its permanent heavenly body by the exertion of His own power (Phil. 3:20–21). This new heavenly body, which will no longer be flesh and blood but entirely spiritual in nature, will be our eternal "dwelling from heaven" in which we will be "clothed" in the hereafter (2 Cor. 5:1–4).

"Faithful is He who calls you, and He also will bring it to pass" (5:24)—i.e., just as God has been faithful to those whom He has called (and who have rightly responded to that call in obedient faith), so He also will usher these same people into glory. The "it" here is this sanctification and preservation that Paul just mentioned (in 5:23). You and I cannot bring "it" to pass; we are simply incapable of such power or ability. But God can and will bring this to pass, provided we remain faithful to the gospel that we had once believed (1 Cor. 15:1–2, Col. 1:22–23).

Paul concludes this epistle with general comments and personal remarks. "Brethren, pray for us" (5:25)—a request he has made on other occasions (Eph. 6:18, Col. 4:3, etc.). The "us" refers to himself, Silvanus, and Timothy, but can easily extend to all men and women who are serving as missionaries and devoting their lives to the cause of Christ's gospel (1 Cor. 16:15–16, Heb. 13:18). Paul strongly believes in the power of prayer, and the benefit that it brings not only to himself but also to those who look beyond their own circumstances to beseech God on behalf of someone else. Thus, he implores Christians everywhere "to strive together with me in your prayers to God for me" (Rom. 15:30).

"Greet all the brethren with a holy kiss" (5:26)—this is a custom among the early Christians, in which men kiss men on the cheek and women kiss women in the same way.[79] It is mentioned several times in the NT (Rom. 16:16, 1 Cor. 16:20, and 2 Cor. 13:12). Western culture has modified this custom to a handshake, but the *principle* of the greeting must remain the same: it must be "holy," that is, without deception, false pretense, or any unholy fellowship. (For an opposite example, think of Judas' kiss when he betrayed the Lord in the garden of Gethsemane.) Greeting one another with a kiss was a normalized custom of the ancient world; but to make it *holy* took this simple greeting to an entirely new and unprecedented level.

"I adjure you by the Lord to have this letter read to all the brethren" (5:27)—Paul adds this instruction to prevent any shielding of anyone in the Thessalonian church from hearing everything he has to say. This seems especially true regarding those matters sensitive to this group, namely, teachings on the Second Coming, the resurrection, and the need to continue in one's responsibilities rather than sitting around and waiting for Jesus to appear. "Adjure" is a strong word that places the person *being* adjured under (a divine) oath, as the Jews did with Jesus (Mat. 26:63). Thus, Paul is pointed in his instruction; there can be no mistaking it. This reading is to be aloud (verbally) in the company of the entire congregation ("in the church," as in Col. 4:16).

"The grace of our Lord Jesus Christ be with you" (5:28)—a standard but sincere benediction with which Paul often opens and/or closes his epistles. The Christian's spiritual well-being is entirely dependent upon God's grace—His forgiveness, blessings, providential oversight, and guidance—and Paul wants this fact understood in the fullest measure.

79 JFB, *Commentary* (electronic), on 5:26.

This provides an excellent parting thought for any correspondence between Christians.

The Second Epistle to the Thessalonians

Salutation and Opening Remarks (2 Thess. 1:1–12)

Paul's opening salutation (1:1–2) is word for word identical with that of *1 Thessalonians,* until he adds in the present epistle "from God the Father and the Lord Jesus Christ" on the end of "Grace to you and peace." (See comments on 1 Thess. 1:1) Likewise, Paul commends the Thessalonians for their love, faith, and endurance amid persecutions (1:3–4), just as he did in the opening comments of his first epistle to them. In fact, *despite* the persecutions, their faith and love continued to grow and excel. Thus, it is "only fitting" for Paul to recognize and give thanks to God for such conduct, since it so appropriately represents the model behavior for believers everywhere. Thus, he (again) boasts about the Thessalonians "among the churches of God" in every place, particularly in Macedonia and Achaia (see 1 Thess. 1:7).[80]

A Church under Attack (1:4–5): The "persecutions and afflictions" (1:4) to which Paul refers would be those inflicted by unbelieving Jews, as described in Acts 17:1–9.[81] It is true that many people in the centuries after the church was established did horrible things to Jews and other ethnic groups in the name of Christ, and there remains no justification for this. At the same time, we should not forget that the first persecution of Christians came from the very people among whom Christ walked, taught, and sought to save.

Jewish opposition to the gospel of Christ was tenacious among the new churches, since the Jews saw "the Way" (Acts 9:1–2) as blasphemous to the Law of Moses and something they had to eradicate (Acts 22:3–5,

80 "Churches of God" would be an acceptable designation for genuinely Christian churches today; in fact, it is used far more often in the NT than any other collective form of identification of the churches. "Churches of Christ" is used once (Rom. 16:16); "church(es) of God" is used eleven times.

81 "Afflictions is a wider term [than "persecutions"—MY WORDS] and includes the painful effects of the persecutions, many of which persist long after the persecution dies down" (Lenski, *Interpretation,* 381).

26:9–11). For the ethnic Jew, there simply is no peaceful coexistence between Judaism and Christianity: he can only choose to follow one or the other. Furthermore, the Jews in Paul's day did not seem to care when Gentiles believed in pagan idolatry, but they became enraged and violent when these same Gentiles chose to believe in Jesus Christ.

Thus, Jesus' prediction came true: "If they persecuted Me, they will also persecute you; if they kept My word, they will keep yours also. But all these things they will do to you for My name's sake, because they do not know the One who sent Me" (John 15:20–21). Likewise, He said: "They will make you outcasts from the synagogue, but an hour is coming for everyone who kills you to think that he is offering service to God. These things they will do because they have not known the Father or Me" (John 16:2–3).

"{This is} a plain indication of God's righteous judgment" (1:5)—the words "this is" are not in the original text but are necessarily implied. Paul sees the suffering of the righteous at the hands of the wicked as an inevitable result of the coexistence of the two groups. The righteous and the wicked cannot live together in the same realm without a pronounced antagonism between the two of them. Just as the Holy Spirit stands in sharp contradiction to carnal behavior (Gal. 5:16), so the Christian stands opposed to the wicked. It is the wicked, however, that actively persecute the righteous, not the other way around. And one defining quality of those "worthy of the kingdom of God" is that they *choose* to suffer such injustices for the Lord's sake. In fact, it is necessary that they choose this route, as the following passages teach:

- "Blessed are those who have been persecuted for the sake of righteousness, for theirs is the kingdom of heaven. Blessed are you when people insult you and persecute you, and falsely say all kinds of evil against you because of Me" (Mat. 5:10–11).
- "The Spirit Himself testifies with our spirit that we are children of God, and if children, heirs also, heirs of God and fellow heirs with Christ, if indeed we suffer with Him so that we may also be glorified with Him" (Rom. 8:16–17).

- "[I have suffered the loss of all things] that I may know Him and the power of His resurrection and the fellowship of His sufferings, being conformed to His death..." (Phil. 3:10, bracketed words added).
- "For ... if when you do what is right and suffer for it you patiently endure it, this finds favor with God" (1 Peter 2:20).

To clarify, no one becomes worthy only *because* he suffers persecution. In fact, suffering for what is not for Christ's name's sake or the sake of righteousness is of no value (cf. 1 Peter 2:20 and 4:15). But even those who suffer for Christ are not earning their way to heaven; worthiness is not determined by human effort, but only by human faith. Thus, "worthy of the kingdom" does not mean "you've earned your way into the kingdom through your suffering," but rather (in so many words) "God sees the worthiness and genuineness of *your faith* because of your choosing to suffering for His kingdom."

Christ's Future Retribution to Be Revealed (1:6–10): Yet, in time, "God's righteous judgment" will bring relief to the righteous who have suffered at the hands of their enemies, and punishment to those who have caused the suffering (1:6–7a). In both cases, justice will be served: the righteous will be vindicated, and the wicked will be sentenced. "For after all it is only just for God to repay with affliction those who afflict you, and ... relief [lit., rest] to you"—i.e., God's recompense is His righteous response to the situation. To "repay with affliction" means that God Himself will deliver divine judgment against those who mistreat His people. Divine judgment is a matter of divine justice: God is the only One capable of rendering such justice without bias, conflicts of interest, or self-serving motives. All this is reminiscent of Joshua's words to Achan: "Why have you troubled us? The LORD will trouble you this day" (Josh. 7:25).

But *when* will this happen? Paul answers this immediately: "when the Lord Jesus will be revealed from heaven" (1:7b). Some people tie this together with what Jesus said to His disciples in Mat. 24, yet this revelation of Jesus of which Paul speaks cannot be the same judgment scenario described there (in Mat. 24:30–31), since the context is completely different. In Mat. 24, Jesus spoke specifically about His vengeance against Jerusalem (i.e., Israel) for their rejection of Him as their King (Luke 19:11–27, 41–44, and 21:20–24). He said nothing of compensation for the persecution of the righteous, only that He will preserve the righteous from being swept up in that judgment.

The present text (1:7), however, has nothing to do with a judgment against Jerusalem, but against those who persecute Christ's church. Furthermore, the "coming" of the Son of Man in Mat. 24 is figurative: Jesus did not literally appear in the sky with power and glory; the sun and moon were not literally darkened; stars did not literally fall from the sky; etc. Yet Paul's depiction of Christ's judgment against the enemies of His church uses no such figurative language. The context is literal and historical—the suffering as well as its "retribution" (compensation or payback). We have no reason to accept Paul's words as anything other than an inspired prediction of a literal future event.

Christ's future appearance will be "from heaven," since this is where He is right now (Col. 3:2). a A heavenly host of angels will accompany Him; He will reveal Himself as the Commander of this great army (as depicted symbolically in Rev. 19:11–16). His appearance will also be "in flaming fire," since fire (as an element of either purification or destruction) often accompanies divine judgment (see Dan. 7:9–10, Heb. 10:27, 12:29, and 2 Pet 3:7).[82] He will "appear a second time for salvation…to those who eagerly await Him" (Heb. 9:28), but He will be "dealing out retribution [vengeance]" to those who stand opposed to Him (1:8). This latter group includes:

- **"those who do not know God"**: Specifically, this refers to Gentiles who stand outside of God's grace because of their ignorance and carnal lusts (Eph. 4:17–19). But it can just as easily refer to Jews who

---

82 Fire is also a characteristic of the Divine Presence of God, as used in OT prophetic writings; thus, some commentators restrict *this* fire (in 1:7) to the manifestation of Christ in glory, with no reference to a destructive fire against the world or the ungodly (Gloag, *Pulpit Commentary*, 3). Yet, the context specifically talks about *divine vengeance*, and not merely Christ's appearance. It stands to reason, then, that the fire mentioned here is not used in a passive sense, but an active one: Christ's appearance is to bring judgment and destruction to those who rejected Him, and the fire that accompanies Him is part of that judgment and destruction (as in Isa. 66:15–16).

assumed a relationship with the Father even though they do not know His Son. Jesus said of them that *because* they do not know the Son, then neither do they know the Father (John 8:41–47, 16:1–3); thus, they are "the false circumcision" (Phil. 3:2) and a "synagogue of Satan" (Rev. 2:9). The context necessarily implies a deliberate choice not to learn of God and/or His Son, for whatever reason, and not an insuperable or insurmountable situation.[83] To "know God" here means to have a covenant relationship with Him through Christ; those outside of that covenant do *not* know Him.

- **"those who do not obey the gospel of our Lord Jesus"**: While those in the first group are condemned because they refused to *learn* of God, people in this second group are condemned because they refused to *obey* that which they had learned. It is true that anyone in the first group also stands guilty of disobedience to God: those who do not *know* God cannot *obey* Him. However, this latter group *had* such a relationship but did not remain true to their covenant promises. This refers to Christians who have not kept the faith and have abandoned their original allegiance to Christ (see Heb. 6:4–6 and 2 Peter 2:20–22).[84]

"These will pay the penalty" (1:9)—"these" referring to people in either group mentioned in the preceding verse. All people in both groups are unbelieving, disobedient, and in rebellion to God; all such people fall under His divine condemnation. God's wrath will be carried out against those who stand opposed to His Son, whether in pursuit of something else or in impenitent disobedience to Him. Paul's use of "eternal destruction" necessarily implies two things: a state of being that will be *unchanged* in nature (thus, "eternal"); and a *punishment* of some kind, but

83 Those who are *unable* to know (specific information) about God or Christ are not exceptions to this scenario but are in a different scenario altogether. Those whose circumstances literally prevented them from such knowledge cannot be held accountable for something outside of their control; yet these will be judged by what they *did* know, and what they *should* have known (Rom. 1:18–20, 2:12–16).

84 Robertson, for one, simply separates the two groups in the most general sense as Gentiles and Jews (*Word Pictures*, 44). In the most basic sense, it is likely that Paul means this as well. However, we cannot help but carry this beyond the situation of Paul's day into the one we face today in which there are many Christians (whose ethnicities are irrelevant) who also fit this description.

not one that leads to annihilation.[85] (A literal annihilation of a human soul is completely foreign to Scripture.)

"Away from the presence of the Lord and...power" defines (in general) the context of this "destruction": the human soul, cut off from all the blessings of and communication with its Creator, will suffer an unspeakably awful existence. In a real sense, God will grant to that soul what it sought in this life—a self-determined existence—and it will forever regret that decision. What the disobedient soul sought, God will finalize; thus, "Depart from Me, accursed ones" (Mat. 25:41). God's grace will no longer be available to such souls; all hope of repentance, redemption, and salvation will be gone.

Whatever else will happen to the soul in that condition, Paul does not specifically say in the present passage (1:8–9). But in all references to the eternal disposition of the ungodly, there is always the idea of punishment involved, whether stated specifically (Mat. 25:46) or by implication (Mat. 8:12). A soul cast into the "outer darkness" and (thus) forever separated from its Source of life is sufficient to bring about its unspeakable suffering. This does not mean, however, that the lost soul will not experience other forms of literal punishments as well.

"When He comes ... on that day" (1:10) provides the contextual timestamp for this fiery judgment and the subsequent destruction of the ungodly. The "when" is defined by an event (Christ's appearance in the sky), not a specific date. This event will usher in the actual salvation of the righteous as well as the judgment of the disbelieving and disobedient. Christ will be glorified "in His saints [or, in the person of His saints]," meaning: He will be honored through the faithful devotion

85 The word "eternal" has been sharply questioned by those who cannot reconcile an *eternal* punishment for crimes committed in a *finite* or *limited* context (i.e., the earthly life). This disagreement has more to do with one's view of God's divine justice than it does the translation of a single word. Nonetheless, in Mat. 25:46, for example, "eternal punishment" for the wicked is mentioned alongside of "eternal life" for the righteous—and "eternal" comes from the same word (*aionios*) as used in 2 Thess. 1:9. In the 66 times this Greek word is used in the NT (in the NASB), it is translated "eternal," "everlasting," or "forever" (*New American Standard Hebrew, Aramaic, and Greek Dictionaries*, Robert L. Thomas, ed., electronic edition [©1988 The Lockman Foundation], G166).

of His saints (Christians) despite their having suffered at the hands of the ungodly for that decision (1 Peter 1:7).

When Christ appears, unbelievers will shrink back in horror at His fiery presentation (cf. Rev. 6:15–17), since this will signal their demise. Yet, Christ will "be marveled at among all who have believed"[86]—i.e., Christians will "marvel" or be amazed with profound wonder at the same sight, since this will signal the end of all their suffering and their entrance into heavenly glory. Thus, the same scene will be an occasion of terror and death for one group but an occasion of victory and joy for the other (cf. 2 Cor. 2:15–16).

"For our testimony to you was believed"—i.e., you (Thessalonians) will share in that joyous marveling because you loved Him before ever having seen Him (1 Pet. 1:8–9). Those who have loved Christ's first appearance long to see His second appearance (2 Tim. 4:8); thus, we are "looking for and hastening the coming of the day of God" (2 Pet. 3:12).

If we combine 1 Thess. 4:13–18 with 2 Thess. 1:6–10 (and passages cited in comments on these two passages), we see that:

- Christ will be revealed from heaven at some future time. This so-called Second Coming will bring the world to an end, meaning that the present physical system will not only cease to operate but will be destroyed as well.[87]

86 Lenski rightly draws attention to the word "all"—meaning, *all* believers of *all* time will see the Lord, not just the Thessalonians (*Interpretation*, 390). This also defeats an alleged figurative "revelation" of Christ that is explained through some natural means of defeat for the Jews (sickness, disease, invasion, war, etc.). Instead, *all* who have suffered for His name's sake will rejoice at His revelation, regardless of time, history, generation, or geography.

87 Some will disagree: "Just because Christ returns does not mean the world will end or be literally destroyed." My response is: then what *does* it mean? If Christ takes into glory all those who have believed in Him, and sends into "eternal destruction" all those who have disbelieved or disobeyed Him, then who is left on the earth? What purpose would there be to even *have* an earth? The opportunity for redemption will be over; all of Christ's enemies will be vanquished (1 Cor. 15:23–26). God can speak the physical world *out* of existence just as easily as He spoke it *into* existence. But some insist that we will dwell upon this earth after it has been rejuvenated and returned to an Eden-like state of being. While fanciful, there is nothing in Scripture to support this. Those who

- At this Coming:
  - The dead in Christ will be raised from their tombs.
  - Those who remain alive in Christ will be taken up into heaven.
  - Those who died outside of Christ will be raised to judgment (John 5:28–29, Acts 24:15).
  - Those who remain alive outside of Christ will be destroyed with a fiery retribution and then will stand judgment before Christ (Luke 19:27, in principle).
  - This fiery retribution will be the same fire that engulfs and destroys the entire world (2 Peter 3:10)—or so it appears.
- All of humanity will stand before the Creator and be ushered into eternal life or eternal judgment (a scene symbolically portrayed in Rev. 20:11–15; see 2 Cor. 5:10).
- All of Christ's enemies will be destroyed (1 Cor. 15:23–26), every knee will bow, and every mouth will be made to confess Him to be Lord over all (Phil. 2:9–11).
- After this, the righteous will enter eternal glory *with* God, and the wicked will enter eternal separation *from* God. The coexistence of the righteous and the wicked, as what we presently have on the earth, will no longer continue but will end forever.

Paul's Prayer for the Thessalonians (1:11–12): Paul's prayer is that the Thessalonians *will* share in the glory he has just described (1:11). Thus, he prays that they will remain faithful to Christ and unshaken by whatever threats or hardships they must face for His name. "[T]hat our God will count you worthy of your calling"—their conduct must remain consistent with the holy calling with which God called them (recall comments on 1:5; see also Eph. 4:1, Phil. 1:27, Col. 1:10, etc.). "If their Lord is to be glorified in them at his Advent [i.e., Second Coming], he must be glorified in their present way of life."[88]

Paul also prays that whatever "good" the Thessalonians desire to perform, God will provide the means and opportunity to do it. Likewise, he prays that their "work of faith"—whatever effort they exert toward

---

die "in the Lord" will be taken into His world; He will not keep us in this one forever.

88 Bruce, *WBC*, 157; bracketed words are mine.

the cause of Christ—will be effectual and productive because of God's power (Eph. 3:20, Heb. 13:20–21). "[S]o that…Jesus will be glorified in you, and you in Him" (1:12)—i.e., Christ will be honored through the faithful devotion of His saints, but also His saints will be honored by Christ (1 Peter 5:6).[89] All such honor will be made possible "according to the grace of our God and…Christ"—i.e., no amount of human effort, works, or faith can make any person worthy of divine honor. Whatever we do remains meaningless unless accompanied by God's grace to compensate for our gross inadequacies; as Christ said, "apart from Me you can do nothing" (John 15:5).

The "Man of Lawlessness" (2 Thess. 2:1–8)

A Warning to Avoid Being Misled (2:1–2): A natural response to what Paul has just described is: "*When* will Christ come?" He has already stated (in 1 Thess. 5:1–3) the *suddenness* or *unexpectedness* of His return ("like a thief in the night"; "while they are saying, 'Peace and safety!'"). He has also said (in that same passage) that no one can know exactly when Christ will return. But the question of "When?" does not have to request a specific date but can address a much broader, historical, and sequential view of things. In other words, "What will happen *first* to usher in this event?" Concerning the destruction of Jerusalem in AD 70, for example, Jesus admitted that He Himself did not know the day or hour (Mat. 24:36), but He did know details that had to take place prior to that event (Mat. 24:5–21, Luke 21:20–22).

From what follows, it is also clear that Paul has discussed this subject with the Thessalonians beyond what he writes in this epistle. Thus, what is written here is new to us, but to them it is merely a reminder of things already covered (see 2:5). Nonetheless, it appears that some of the Thessalonian Christians have forgotten what Paul said, or in their enthusiasm for Christ's return they have neglected this instruction. Also, there may be some in their number (or from outside their group?) that are putting a tremendous emphasis on this Second Coming to the

89 Consider all the tremendous privileges and honors that Christ promises to the one who "overcomes" in His letters to the seven churches (Rev. 2–3).

exclusion of all other responsibilities. If this is the case, Paul wants to put a stop to this unbecoming behavior.

Thus, in the rest of this epistle, he does not back away for a moment from the reality of what has been said—Christ *is* coming, and believers *will* enter into glory!—but at the same time he warns them against letting these facts cloud their judgment or obscure their moral objectives. Great enthusiasm is one thing, and Paul does not attempt to suppress it; irresponsibility is quite another thing, however, and Paul does not tolerate it for a moment.

"Now ... with regard to the coming [lit., presence] of our Lord Jesus Christ and our gathering together to Him" (2:1) provides the context for this discussion. Thus, Christ's *coming* and the *gathering* of the saints (in the clouds, where He will appear—1 Thess. 4:16–17) speak of the same event: *when* Christ comes, *at that time* we shall be gathered.[90] Paul "requests"—and it is a strong or urgent request—that the Thessalonian Christians not allow themselves to be led to believe that Christ has already come, and that somehow they *missed out* on this event.[91] Paul does not even address the untenable idea that they *could* have missed it, since it is a cataclysmic event that could not possibly *be* missed. Instead, he warns against them being "shaken from [their] composure [or, mentally agitated; emotionally upset]" by false communications. These communications include a:

- **"spirit"**—that is, a person claiming to have a spirit of prophecy. Christians are to "test the spirits [of prophets] to see whether they

90 The Greek word for "gathering" (*episunagoge*) is only in one other place in the NT (Heb. 10:25), in reference to the "gathering" or "assembling together" of the saints. Yet, Heb. 12:23 speaks of the "general assembly" of the saints in an otherworldly context, which sheds light on the present passage.

91 "To reassure them that this is not, in fact, the case, Paul reminds the Thessalonians of two events he had previously told them would occur (cf. 2:5). Since neither had taken place at the time of Paul's writing, it simply was not possible that the day of the Lord had come. The two events are the 'rebellion' and the revelation of the 'man of lawlessness' (2:3). The basic point of this passage is that these two events, which were to take place within history, had not yet occurred and, consequently, the day of the Lord at the end of history could not have occurred, either" (Scott, "Not Grieve as Others," *A Life Worthy*, 235).

are from God, because many false prophets have gone out into the world" (1 John 4:1, bracketed words are mine). Any "spirit" that contradicts what Paul has already said is a false spirit, since he speaks according to Christ's authority.

- **"message"**—a report of some kind given by Paul by way of another party. Whatever message Paul gives on this subject will not contradict what he had already communicated to the Thessalonian Christians.
- **"letter as if from us"**—a specific form of communication allegedly written by Paul or one of his fellow ministers (such as Timothy, Silvanus, etc.). Such correspondence could not be genuine if indeed it claimed that Christ *had* come, when in fact Paul has said otherwise.

Paul uses "coming of our Lord Jesus Christ" (2:1) and "day of the Lord" (2:2) interchangeably here, and therefore must refer to the same occasion or event (see comments on 1 Thess. 5:1–3). The "day of the Lord" (2:2) is a concept rooted in OT prophecy (see Isa. 13:9, 61:1–2, Ezek. 7:19, 30:3, Joel 1:15, 2:11, 2:31, Amos 5:18–20, Zeph. 1:14, Mal. 4:5, etc.).[92] In every case, it referred *at least* to a form of judgment, but in some cases, it *also* indicated a display of God's power to vindicate and/or deliver His people.

In this latter case, the Lord destroyed those who had imprisoned or brought suffering upon His people: He destroyed one group and saved another. Thus, it was a day (occasion) of divine vengeance upon God's enemies, but also a day of redemption for those who trusted in Him. This "day" was accompanied by extraordinary signs (miracles or unprecedented events) or tremendous upheavals (in society, government, religion, or any combination of these).

---

92 "H. Wheeler Robinson sees in this prophetic 'Day' four characteristics—judgment, universality, supernatural intervention and proximity. In addition he notes four features contained in it—it brings to a focus the manifestation of God's purpose in history; it is a day on which God acts and not merely speaks; it is a day on which God is shown to be victorious within this present world-order and on the stage of human history; it is a day which ushers in a new era on the earth" (quoted in D. S. Russell, *Between the Testaments* [Philadelphia: Fortress Press, 1965], 110).

The "day of the Lord" in the NT has carried over these same ideas. The most familiar to us is the fulfillment of Joel's prophecy of the "day of the Lord" in the commencement of Christ's church (compare Joel 2:28–32 and Acts 2:16–21). On that occasion were both miracles *and* great upheaval (for Jews *and* ultimately Gentiles). The "day of the Lord" in the present passage (2:2) will be a *final* "day" (or event) in which Christ will return and bring an end to the "last days" of humanity. After the "last days" end, there will be no more "days," dispensations, or epochs of human history: there will be no *need* for these, nor will there be any *occasion* for these. Every person who has ever lived will have made his (or her) choice as to whether he will serve the Lord. The time for redemption will be over; the opportunity for repentance will have passed; God will finalize each person's decision concerning Him.

The Sequence of Events (2:3–7): "Let no one in any way deceive you" (2:3)—which implies that some will *try* to deceive them, but that they should not fall victim to their lies or false visions.[93] Christ's return will not happen "unless the apostasy comes first"—lit., a falling away (from the faith; from the truth) (1 Tim. 4:1–2, 2 Tim. 4:3–4).[94] This necessarily implies that a significant portion of the visible church on earth will succumb to teachings and deceptions that lead it away from the Lord (Mat. 24:10–13, in principle). In a more general sense, it refers to an abandonment of divine truth itself: people will no longer regard God's word as credible, relevant, or binding.[95]

This also means that there will be a specific sequence of historical events that must take place before Christ will return. Yet this does *not* mean that Christ will return immediately *after* those events have manifested

---

93 "Paul broadens the warning to go beyond conversation and letter. He includes 'tricks' of any kind. It is amazing how gullible some of the saints are when a new deceiver pulls off some stunts in religion" (Robertson, *Word Pictures*, 49).

94 For a further study on the apostasy mentioned in the NT, I strongly recommend my book, *The New Testament Pattern: God's Plan for Christians and Their Churches* (Spiritbuilding Publishers, 2023); go to www.spiritbuilding.com/chad.

95 "Apostasy" is transliterated from *apostasia*, a defection, revolt, or forsaking (of something) (*NAS Dictionaries* [electronic], G646]). Bruce translates this to "rebellion" (*WBC*, 166), and it is, but it is more than just the *act* of rebellion; this rebellion is specifically incited by a rejection of (divine) authority.

themselves, but that He will not come *until* their fulfillment. How much time passes between the prophesied events and His coming is not answered for us here.[96]

Paul describes this so-called "man of lawlessness" (2:3–12) as "the son of destruction [or, perdition]"; "lawless one"; "the one whose coming is in accord with the activity of Satan." All these descriptors refer to the same wicked attributes of this "man." "These terms indicate that he is the very personification and fullness of sin and lawlessness, as Jesus is the personification and fullness of righteousness and truth."[97] "Lawlessness" is sin (1 John 3:4); thus a "man of lawlessness" is a man sold entirely into sin and engaging in sinful activity. This "man" opposes God and everything that God stands for. His self-exaltation relates to worship and religion; in other words, he is not a mere political figure or charismatic leader (2:4). He magnifies himself not only above all the pagan gods of this world but even defies the God of heaven. The "temple of God" is a phrase not used after Acts 2 to refer to the literal temple in Jerusalem, since Christ's church has become the spiritual temple of the Lord (Eph. 2:21). In effect, this "man of lawlessness" defies God through his persecution of Christ's church.[98]

---

96 We can draw from OT history to explain this. Isaiah, for example, prophesied of the Babylonian captivity of the Jews, then their release from that captivity and the subsequent destruction of Babylon. After this, Isaiah spoke of their Messiah ("David," "the Branch," the suffering "Servant," etc.) who would usher in a new age of restoration and glory for the Jews. It might have appeared to the Jews that their Messiah would come *immediately* after the fall of Babylon, since Isaiah did not specify otherwise. Yet, Daniel provides information that clarifies the situation: the Jews *will* be delivered by their Messiah (Christ), but not until the days of the fourth Gentile Empire (Rome). It appears that we are looking at a similar situation for ourselves: the apostles declared that Christ *would* come, but not until certain sequences take place and certain conditions are met first. Thus, like the Jews who waited for Messiah for centuries in the intertestamental period, we also have waited for centuries for history to have run its course and the moral condition of mankind to reach a level of iniquity that warrants a universal judgment (cf. Gen. 15:16).

97 Homer Hailey, "Appendix B: John's Antichrist and Paul's Man of Sin," *A Commentary on Daniel* (Las Vegas: Nevada Publications, 2001), 272.

98 Daniel 8 talks about a "little horn" that will rise out of the Seleucid dynasty of the Greek Empire and exalts himself over God and His people, specifically by desecrating the literal temple in Jerusalem. This can refer to none other than Antiochus IV

This man also will "[display] himself as being God"—not just someone who thinks himself divinely *appointed* (as the kings of Europe would do later in history [a.k.a. "divine right"]), but one who thinks himself *to be* a divine being who possesses god-like power.[99] Paul has obviously said more about this "man of lawlessness" to the Thessalonians in person than what he tells us here (2:5). Yet his present objective is not to revisit the entire discussion, but to remind them that Christ will not come *before* this "man of lawlessness" appears and his rampage against God and His people has run its course.

Paul then turns his discussion toward "what restrains him [the man of lawlessness] now" (2:6). He does not actually *disclose* what restrains him, but something *does* restrain him. In other words, he has not yet come to power; he is not yet able to conduct his ambitious and arrogant crusade against God. "[I]n his time he will be revealed"—that is, according to the allotment of time God has given to him to do his evil work, when all the sequences of other events have run *their* courses, and when all the conditions of the world are optimum for his entrance. Thus, while this "man" has not yet been "revealed" (or, made visible or identifiable), the system of lawlessness which supports him and by which he operates is already in motion.

The "mystery of lawlessness" (2:7) indicates something that is not yet

---

Epiphanes (ruled 175–163 BC). While Paul obviously does not refer to *this* man as the "man of lawlessness," the two have the same character, exhibit the same arrogance, and launch crusades against God's people. Just as that man (Antiochus) was destroyed not by human agency, but a divine curse (Dan. 8:23–25), so the "man of lawlessness" will be destroyed through divine intervention.

99 On the "man of lawlessness" sitting in God's temple, Lenski writes: "This Antichrist reveals himself as the Antichrist by this *pagan* act of seating himself in the *true* God's own sanctuary. He does not deny the true God, he is neither atheist nor agnostic; in fact, he worships the true God. But he does it by this pagan act, the climax of all anti-Christianity. He sits in God's own place as if he, too, were God and shows and exhibits himself to all Christendom with the claim 'that he is God,' that no less than deity belongs also to him. The very idea of extending deity in this way is utterly pagan. The great apostasy accepts this claim and honors this Antichrist with divine honor. That is what constitutes this apostasy. When Paul wrote, the people of God had never seen an apostasy and an Antichrist like this; nor has there been another who is comparable to this one since that time" (*Interpretation*, 411–2).

visible to human sight (or, has not yet become a historical reality). "Mystery," as used elsewhere in the NT, always refers to something that the Holy Spirit has once predicted and then has revealed through His prophets (as in Eph. 3:3–7). This "mystery" obviously involves a system of authority and opportunity that allows this "man" to ascend to self-deification. But it also involves another man ("he")—or possibly a series of men (as a line of rulers)—that currently restrains the "man of lawlessness" but will be removed or overcome for this "man" to triumph over him (or them).

The Destruction of This "Man" and His Followers (2:8–12): What will happen to this "man of lawlessness"? Paul does not hesitate to say: "The Lord will slay [him] with the breath of His mouth and bring [him] to an end by the appearance of His coming" (2:8, bracketed words added). The "appearance" or "coming" of the Lord has already been clearly established (recall 2:1–2): this is none other than Christ's Second Coming when He literally appears in the clouds to bring judgment upon the unbelieving and the disobedient, but righteous vindication to His people (recall 1:6–9). Thus, if the Lord will "slay" this "man of lawlessness" *at the time of His coming,* then this necessarily demands that this "man" will still be upon the earth when Christ returns.

In the previous section (2:1–8), Paul introduced a future "man of lawlessness" who will exalt himself to a god-like status while claiming to have support of God's people on earth. In this present section (2:9–12), Paul further describes this "man's" activity as being in concert with Satan himself—thus, the "man" cannot *be* Satan, since he mentions the two individually in the same context. He (like Satan) will attempt to attract attention and followers through deceptive "power and signs and false miracles [or, lying wonders]" (2:9). Whatever "signs" he performs will have the appearance of genuineness but will be anything but genuine. Instead, these performances will be purposely misleading forgeries (as in Mat. 24:24 and Rev. 13:13–15). This entire charade will be a "deception of wickedness" (2:10a) designed to con and seduce those who have rejected divine truth into believing that he (the "man of lawlessness") is worthy of their devotion and worship.

The critical issue is: what is the *identity* of this "man of lawlessness"? If this "man" will be on the earth when Christ returns, this necessarily puts him in the eschatological period—i.e., in the end-time of human history. Regardless, we might also ask: is it even *possible* for us to know his identity for certain, or is Paul (by inspiration) being purposely obscure in his description of him so that we *cannot* know him by name? Also, is it possible that this "man" is not *one* individual person, but is an office, position, or status that is succeeded by one man after another until the return of Christ? Or is it possible that this "man" *is* an individual person, but (even long after his death) he continues to be the figure of authority and charismatic influence for the religion and believers that follow him throughout history?[100] Theories as to the identity of this "man" include:

- **He is a specific Roman emperor or a characterization of *all* the Roman emperors who persecuted the church through the first, second, and third centuries.** This view is based upon passages in *Daniel* which appear to speak of the same situation (see Dan. 11:36–45). Daniel's prophecy deals with a "king"—really, a series of kings or emperors—during the Roman Empire: "Then the king will do as he pleases, and he will exalt and magnify himself above every god and will speak monstrous things against the God of gods; and he will prosper until the indignation is finished, for that which is decreed will be done" (11:36). It is true that Emperor Domitian (ruled AD 81–96) launched an imperial persecution against Christians (as well as other groups), and regarded himself as a god, insisting that people recognize him as such. And there were several emperors who came after him whose persecution of the church made Domitian's efforts pale in comparison. The problem with this view is that the Roman Empire and its emperors have long since disappeared (see Dan. 7:11), yet Paul says this "man of lawlessness" will be destroyed by Christ at His coming—and "coming" or "appearance" in this context is very specific.

100 Regarding what he calls a "certain reticence" in Paul's explanation, Bruce says that "this can be explained if more explicit language was liable to cause trouble should the letter fall into the wrong hands. In Thessalonica the missionaries [Paul, Silas, etc.—MY WORDS] had been charged with subversion, with proclaiming a rival to the emperor who ruled in Rome. It would be best not to say anything in a letter which could be interpreted as lending color to such a charge" (*WBC*, 176).

- **He is the pope (i.e., papal office) of the Catholic Church.** This view has great popularity, especially among Protestant theologians. And there is much to support it: the popes have historically regarded themselves as the only worthy representatives (vicars) of Christ on earth. When they legislate for the Catholic Church, they allegedly speak with the authority of Christ Himself.[101] The arrogances, corruptions, bogus claims of miracles, and deceptions of the papal office are many, and may be more multiplied than we will ever know. In this view, the (singular) "man of lawlessness" must be identified as an office that is occupied by many different men over time; even so, this does not make this conclusion untenable. It is likely, too, that the Catholic Church and its popes will still be in existence when Christ returns. "[W]hat restrains him now" (from Paul's point in time) would be the Roman Empire itself. When the Empire fell (officially, in the late fifth century), it created a huge power vacuum over much of Europe, Northern Africa, and Palestine. The Church assumed control over much of this, and its jurisdiction became known as the Holy Roman Empire (HRE). The HRE dominated Western Europe throughout the Medieval Era; during that time, the pope had more authority than kings of individual nations. Even though this power has since abated, the pope still wields control over a significant number of people, and he continues to regard himself as God's highest authority on earth. There are some questions that remain regarding this view, but it remains one of the best supported of all the views put forward.[102]
- **He is the Antichrist of Premillennialist doctrine.** In this view, the "man of lawlessness" and the alleged Antichrist/Beast of Rev. 13 are the same. This view is wildly popular among contemporary evangelicals and all those who tend to interpret virtually every prophecy in Scripture as having *something* to do with a future

101 The pope's legislative pronouncements are referred to as *ex cathedra* ("from the chair"), in which he speaks with a divinely-invested authority that is binding upon the "universal church" (i.e., the Catholic Church). Such pronouncements are regarded as infallible and thus "irreformable" by any decision of the church itself ("Ex Cathedra," *Catholic Encyclopedia*, www.newadvent.org; cited December 11, 2013).

102 Coffman, for one, argues this position passionately ("Excursus on 'The Man of Sin,'" *Commentary*, 106–117).

Antichrist and his ushering in the end of the world. Premillennialists believe that the Antichrist is (according to the most popular version of this view) a single global leader who will rule over a ten-nation confederacy that controls the entire world. He will gain power immediately after the alleged Rapture, in which all Christians, both living and dead, will be snatched away from the earth, leaving the rest of the world to endure a godless and church-less existence. Those who become Christians after the Rapture will face a seven-year-long Tribulation period in which they will be the primary targets of the Antichrist's global persecution. At the end of seven years will be a cataclysmic battle (a.k.a. Armageddon) between the forces of evil and Christ's heavenly army. Christ will vanquish the Antichrist, destroy his 200-million-man army, and reign in Jerusalem for a thousand years in a newly built temple of God on the exact site of the original Solomonic temple. This is the basic expectation of Premillennialists, and the "man of lawlessness" seems to fit perfectly into this scenario. The problems, however, are manifold, including the very premise of Premillennialism itself—a doctrine that necessarily implies that Christ failed in His earthly mission and God failed to fulfill completely all His promises to the nation of Israel. This view is easily the least credible of all the views concerning the identity of the "man of lawlessness." In fact, *any* view that necessarily implies that God failed at *anything* but will come back and try again "for real" in the future must be immediately rejected.

- **He is Mohammed (and the religion of Islam).** This view is gaining popularity, especially in recent decades as we witness the explosion of Islam throughout the world.[103] At present, Islam is the fastest growing religion; its adherents, by sheer birthrates alone (assuming their children and children's children remain faithful to this religion) will dominate Europe, Asia, Africa, and possibly the United States within another fifty years. The "man of lawlessness" would *specifically*

103 This is not a new thought, however. In the Middle Ages, "The Greek Church was naturally led to regard the prophecy as a prediction of Mohammedanism [Islam]; the apostasy was the falling away of many Greek and Oriental Churches to Mohammedanism; the man of sin was Mohammed; and the restraining influence the power of the Roman empire" (Gloag, "Excursus on the Man of Sin," *Pulpit Commentary*, 54; bracketed word is mine).

be Mohammed himself, since he claimed to be God's only worthy spokesman and thus greater in authority than Jesus Christ. His religion claims to be tolerant of the Christian faith, but in fact Islam is not truly tolerant of *any* religion except its own. Muslims claim to be loyal to Allah (their version of the God of the OT) and will kill others in His name, but in fact they are in complete rebellion to God's Son (see John 16:2–3). What kept Mohammed—really, anyone *like* Mohammed—at bay in Paul's lifetime was again the Roman Empire. Once this restraint was removed, the door was open for all sorts of charismatic leaders, religious and otherwise, to lead people astray. As for signs and false miracles, Muslims will claim that the production of the Quran itself is a miracle, but otherwise they do not seem to rely upon miracles to the extent that Catholicism does. This seems to be the weakest aspect of this position.

- ☐ **He is someone who has not yet been revealed to history, but who will be revealed in our future.** As usual, one's own generation tends to believe that it has already seen everything that could possibly happen in the world, and some believe that we (whoever "we" are) are always on the brink of The End. (Someday, these people will be right!) But it is also presumptuous for us to think that what Paul foretold has already happened or has already happened in the way we *expected* it to happen. Perhaps someone or something will arise in our future that will completely overwhelm anything we have yet experienced to fulfill Paul's predictions. Perhaps, too, there is good reason why the Holy Spirit was *not* specific when He inspired Paul to write about this "man of lawlessness." In fact, there have been *many* lawless men (who claimed to have divine power and/or authority) throughout history. It is possible that the Holy Spirit did not tell us about any *one* "man," but that many would come in this same guise and speak these same arrogant words. Just as before the destruction of Jerusalem, so the "man of lawlessness"—whether a single man, a position held by men, or a religion begun by men (or a man)—will continue to raise his ugly head until the end of the world: "Many false prophets will arise and will mislead many," and lawlessness will "increase" because of them (Mat. 24:11–12).

- **He is the personification of evil and is otherwise described as the "Gog and Magog" of Rev. 20.** This is a view that Homer Hailey maintained, and I believe him to be on the right track.[104] If you compare what is said of the "man of lawlessness" in 2 Thess. 2 and the "Gog and Magog" of Rev. 20:7–10, there is a conspicuous and unavoidable similarity between the two.[105] (This also corresponds to the description of "Gog and Magog" in Ezek. 38, which describes not actual nations but a character of a godless horde of people that attempt to destroy God's people.) In this case, the so-called "man of lawlessness" is in fact many people, and such people will certainly continue to defraud, deceive, mislead, misinform, and exploit many others, and especially those who choose to remain gullible in their thinking and naïve about God. Before Jesus returns, this horde of ungodly people will rise as one person and attempt to destroy God's people, just as we see in Ezek. 38. And, just as in Ezekiel's prophecy, God (Christ) will personally intervene and destroy this "Gog and Magog"/"man of lawlessness" finally.

Christ will destroy the "man of lawlessness," but He will also destroy those who succumb to his lies, fraudulence, and arrogant teachings. "Those who perish" (2:10) refers to those seduced by the "deception of wickedness" provided by the "man of lawlessness." To "perish" in this context must refer to those who will not be saved (as in John 3:16, 1 Cor. 1:18, 15:18, 2 Cor. 4:3, etc.), not to those who merely lose their physical lives.

In other words, these people who swallow the lies and deceptions of the "man of lawlessness" forfeit their souls in the process. Since "they did not receive the love of the truth," they render themselves unable to discern truth from error. It is not that they did not have "the truth" made available to them; rather, they purposely or carelessly rejected it, and in the process made themselves completely insensitive to the gospel of salvation. "Not only did they not receive the truth when it was offered

104 See Hailey, "Appendix B," *Daniel*, 272–280.

105 If we take the "temple of God" (2 Thess. 2:4) metaphorically, as depicting Christ's church (as a temple; cp. Eph. 2:19–21), and the "camp of the saints" (Rev. 20:9) as referring to the same group of people, this picture becomes clear.

them, but, what was worse, they were destitute even of a love of the truth."[106]

When people choose to "pay attention to deceitful spirits and doctrines of demons" (1 Tim. 4:1) instead of seeking the truth, God *does not stop them* from their downward spiral into moral darkness. "God will send upon them a deluding influence..." (2:11)—this cannot mean that God forces such people into spiritual ruin, for this contradicts everything we know about God's nature and intentions as derived from the Scriptures (John 3:16, Luke 19:10, 1 Tim. 2:4, etc.).

What Paul says here is parallel to what he has said elsewhere when people turn away from God in disbelief and ingratitude: God "[gives] them over" to their own lusts, dishonor, depravity, degrading passions, and unholy behaviors (Rom. 1:22–32). This "deluding influence" [lit., a working of error] does not originate *from* God, but He allows it to come upon them; He does not prevent them from sinking ever deeper into their moral abyss.

> When Pharaoh hardens his heart ..., God hardens Pharaoh's heart (Exod. 9:12). When the king of Israel hates God's true prophets, then the Lord permits him to be deceived by placing a lying spirit in the mouth of other prophets (2 Chron. 18:22). When men practice impurity, God gives them up in the lusts of their hearts to impurity (Rom. 1:24, 26). And when they stubbornly refuse to acknowledge God, he finally gives them up to a base mind and to unclean behavior (Rom. 1:28).[107]

God does not deceive anyone: His word is truth (John 17:17) and He Himself is Light (1 John 1:5). Everything about God is holy, pure, and righteous; "Every good thing given and every perfect gift is from above, coming down from the Father of lights, with whom there is no variation or shifting shadow" (James 1:17). God does not tempt people to sin (James 1:13–16), but He does not prevent people from sinning, either. Sin is a choice, never something imposed upon us; our sin is

106 Gloag, *Pulpit Commentary*, 26.

107 Hendriksen, *NTC*, 186.

our responsibility, not something conferred upon us by someone else's actions or responsibility. God does allow us to be tempted but does not force us to choose error over truth. Thus, this "deluding influence" indicates something that God no longer *restrains* from overcoming those who persistently refuse to believe in Him.

As a result of their own decision to reject the truth, such people "will believe what is false"—that is, they will make no distinction between satanic lies and heavenly truth.[108] The *purpose* for God's having allowed such people to believe in error is so that He can judge them fairly: they had opportunity to believe the truth, but they voluntarily and persistently rejected it (2:12). If He had never given them access to the truth, or if He had never allowed them their own decision concerning it, then His punishment of them would be unjust. As it is, however, the punishment *is* just, and God is innocent of any injustice.

Since these people "exchanged he truth of God for a lie" (Rom. 1:25), they "repudiate it and judge [themselves] unworthy of eternal life" (Acts 13:46). The fact that they "took pleasure in wickedness" underscores the deliberate intent or personal decision made in the matter: wickedness did not enter their heart against their will, but they *enjoyed* it and thus *pursued* it, and even gave hearty *approval* to it (Rom. 1:32). They followed the lusts and sensuous cravings of their heart, and these led them away from God's light and into Satan's dominion of darkness (Acts 26:18).

Concerning this "man of lawlessness," then, we can conclude from the passage, from Paul's own perspective of time:

- A general apostasy (i.e., a falling away from divinely revealed truth; an abandonment of God's word) will occur, likely well *beyond* Paul's lifetime.
- The seeds of this apostasy (that will usher in the "man of lawlessness"), however, are already developing *during* Paul's lifetime.

---

108 This is not a new phenomenon. God said to ancient Israel: "Woe to those who call evil good, and good evil; who substitute darkness for light and light for darkness; who substitute bitter for sweet and sweet for bitter!" (Isa. 5:20).

- ❑ A restraining power or person prevents the apostasy (and thus the "man") at the time of Paul's writing.
- ❑ The Thessalonians have been told who (or what) this restraining power is.
- ❑ The "man of lawlessness" will publicly reveal himself once this restraint is removed.
- ❑ This "man" will (figuratively) sit in the temple of God and will oppose Him, exalt himself, and claim divine privileges. The "temple" in this context refers to Christ's church on earth: the "man" will viciously persecute Christians as a means of establishing and increasing his own power.
- ❑ He is not Satan himself, but he acts in full compliance with Satan's will.
- ❑ He will exercise false signs that many people will regard to be genuine miracles.
- ❑ He will deceive those who have rejected God's truth and have embraced lies and deceptions as though they *are* truth.
- ❑ Christ will destroy him (or his religion; his successors) upon His cosmic appearance, the Second Coming.

Commendation and Admonition (2 Thess. 2:13–3:5)

God's Call of His Beloved People (2:13–17): Paul abruptly ends his description of those who revel in lies and wickedness. Instead, he wants to praise the genuineness and godliness of the Thessalonian believers. "But we should always give thanks to God for you" (2:13) echoes what Paul has already said (recall 1:3; see also 1 Thess. 1:2–3): the Thessalonians are often on Paul's mind and therefore in his prayers to God. His identifying them as "beloved by the Lord" is in sharp contrast to those whom God will judge as evil men who follow the "man of lawlessness" (or any wicked leadership).

"God has chosen you from the beginning for salvation" (2:13)—this sounds at first to support Calvinism, which claims that God has chosen the salvation of every person before he was ever born (known as "unconditional election"). But while Calvinism focuses on the alleged choosing (or election) of *individual* believers, Paul consistently refers to God's having chosen the *collective* of believers—i.e., Christ's church in general (Rom. 8:29–30, Eph. 1:4–7, 2 Tim. 2:10, Titus 1:1, etc.; see also Rev. 17:14). We have no reason to believe that God hand-picked specific Thessalonians for salvation (and thus decreed for others to be lost eternally); however, it is entirely appropriate to view God's predestination of Christ's church for salvation. (No doubt God foresaw the existence of a specific congregation in the city of Thessalonica.) But, as to who would belong to this body of believers—and who would reject such opportunity—is determined by individual free will, not a divine sovereign decree.

- "The beginning" can refer to *the* beginning (i.e., in the eternity before God made the world; see Eph. 3:11–12 and 2 Tim. 1:8–9, for example); or the beginning of Christ's church, since the Thessalonians are first generation believers. Either answer is applicable.[109] Paul thus contrasts two groups: those condemned for rejecting the truth, and those saved because they have received the truth. In both cases, people made voluntary decisions to follow one power or the other—either the power of Satan leading to spiritual ruin or the power of God leading to spiritual life.
- "Through [or, in] sanctification by the Spirit"—see comments on 1 Thess. 4:7–8. Christians are called (or invited) for the purpose of being set apart to perform good works for God (Mat. 5:16, Eph. 2:10). The initial occasion for this sanctification was at the time of their "washing" or baptism (1 Cor. 6:11, Eph. 5:25–27, and Titus 3:4–5). The Holy Spirit is always directly involved in the sanctification of the believer's soul: Christ's blood is necessary to atone for sin, and the Holy Spirit's sanctification is necessary for

109 "In Greek the expression 'from the beginning' (*ap archēs*) could have easily been confused for the Greek word for 'first fruits' (*aparchēn*), or vice versa. (In the early manuscripts no space was left between the words.) The first reading looks legitimate because it was customary for the NT writers (especially Paul) to speak of God's choosing his elect from the beginning, even before the foundation of the world (see Eph. 1:4; 2 Tim. 1:9). The second reading also seems genuine because Paul had the habit of calling the first converts (in certain geographical regions) the 'first fruits' (see Rom. 16:5; 1 Cor. 16:15). Nevertheless, most modern translations contain the first reading and note the second in the margin" (JFB, *Commentary*, on 2:13).

preparing that soul to enter God's service. Christ's atonement by blood *and* the Spirit's sanctification work together in one's "born again" transformation from a sinner to a child of God (1 Peter 1:2–3).

- "And faith in the truth"—the Spirit's role is to sanctify and lead the believer (Gal. 5:16); the believer's role is to demonstrate faith in what God has said He will do for him (i.e., His truth). God chooses believers by offering them the gospel; those who accept this offer are to supply their faith with whatever it needs to survive (2 Pet. 1:5–11). A believer cannot sanctify himself to God, and the Holy Spirit does not have faith for the believer. Rather, God does His part that the believer cannot do, and he (or she) is to do his part that God does not do. God's work (grace) and the believer's confidence in God (faith) are the two bookends of one's salvation.

"It was for this [i.e., to be sanctified by the Holy Spirit] He called you through our gospel" (2:14, bracketed words added)—now Paul provides the *method* and *purpose* of God's "calling" people into His church:

- The ***method*** is through the preaching of the gospel (Rom. 10:17). There is no record in the NT of a single person being saved (becoming a Christian) without first hearing and then obediently responding to the same gospel that Paul preached (Eph. 1:13–14, Col. 1:3–6). Furthermore, no one is saved only because a miracle was performed upon them or for their benefit. People must hear the word of God—the message of truth—and then they must respond in obedience to it (think of Cornelius and company in Acts 10). In other words, God provides the basis for our faith—the reason and evidence for it—but He does not actually *save* us until we provide for Him the substance of our faith. "By this we know that we have come to know Him, if we keep His commandments" (1 John 2:3)—and these commandments are in the gospel message of salvation. Such commandments are as necessary for *becoming* a Christians as they are for *living* as a Christian thereafter.
- The ***purpose*** is for sanctification—the act of making people holy and consecrated to fulfill God's will through their service and self-sacrifice. Under the Law of Moses, sacrifices for sin were offered

> first, then burnt offerings for consecration—always in this order. No one can be consecrated whose sins remain; yet God expects one whom He has forgiven to consecrate himself (through the sacrificial process) for His service. Sanctification, then, is not an empty formality but serves a most important purpose. Christ forgives people *for a purpose*—not only to save their souls but also to bring them into service in God's kingdom. Those who refuse to serve in this way also forfeit their salvation, since service is one of the conditional premises *of* salvation.

"That you may gain the glory of our Lord Jesus Christ" (2:14)—a reference (in the context of this epistle) to the Second Coming, when Christ appears in His glory (recall 1:6–9 and 2:1–2). Those sanctified by God will also be prepared for Christ's return, if indeed they remain faithful to their calling until their deaths (Col. 1:21–23, Rev. 2:10). Upon His appearance, those who have died "in the Lord" (Rev. 14:13) will be raised to glory, their physical bodies having been "sown" (buried) in dishonor (see 1 Cor. 15:36–49). Those who are still alive will be caught up to Him in the clouds: "we will not all sleep, but we will all be changed" (1 Cor. 15:51–52). Thus, those whose faith in God endures through this life "may be found to result in praise and glory and honor at the revelation of Jesus Christ" (1 Peter 1:7).

To participate in this glory, then, believers must "stand firm" in their faith (2:15)—an admonition found frequently in Paul's epistles (Eph. 6:11–14; see notes on 1 Thess. 3:8). They must also "hold to the traditions" given them by apostolic authority. The word "tradition" here is from *paradosis*, which means an instruction, narrative, precept, etc. that has been handed over to another by way of speaking or writing.[110] In the present context, this instruction is the apostolic teachings which Paul has provided the Thessalonians in person ("by word of mouth") or through his epistles ("by letter").

This is the same instruction which Paul has taught in every church (1 Cor. 4:17) and carries the authority of earlier prophets of God and

110 Thayer, *Lexicon* (electronic), G3862]. "The worth of the tradition lies not in the form but in the source and the quality of the content" (Robertson, *Word Pictures*, 55).

the teaching of Christ Himself (2 Pet. 3:1–2), since these all originate from the Holy Spirit of God. Paul implies here that at least some of the Thessalonians have been led astray from his original instruction, possibly because of a letter written by someone else, or a forgery of his own letter (recall 2:2). This is stronger language than what he used in the first letter since the problem among them has still not been resolved.

While Paul needs the Thessalonians to stand firm in their faith and continue in the apostolic teaching, he does not leave their salvation to their own efforts. Instead, he defers to God's power, grace, and divine providence to guide them to that end (2:16–17). "Our Lord Jesus Christ" and "God our Father" are both portrayed as working in seamless cooperation toward the same goal: the salvation of those who call upon them for help. Both the Son and the Father have proven their love for us—the Father through sending His Son as our Savior, and the Son for serving as a sacrifice for our sins—and in them we have "eternal comfort" and "good hope by grace." The eternal comfort is the confidence and consolation we have in God because of the surety of His salvation. Our "good hope" rests upon divine grace: God doing everything for us that we cannot do for our salvation. It is only through this love, comfort, hope, grace, and strength that the believer will overcome this world *and* be able to fulfill his work of service to God. This hymn-like exhortation is reminiscent of Rom. 16:25–27, Eph. 3:14–21, Heb. 13:20–21, and Jude 1:24–25.

Paul Asks for Their Prayers and Continued Obedience (3:1–5): Paul has gone to great lengths to inspire, encourage, and admonish the Thessalonians; now he calls upon them to help *him*. "Finally, brethren, pray for us" (3:1–2)—Paul has often requested prayers on his behalf from various groups of Christians (Rom. 15:30, Eph. 6:18–19, Col. 4:2–4, 1 Thess. 5:25, etc.). When Christians pray for one another (rather than for themselves), they become more involved in the ministry of the kingdom of God rather than simply seeking their own welfare. Specifically, Paul requests prayers for the Thessalonians to share the gospel with other men and women, in the same manner that Paul shared it with them.

Instead of being satisfied with what has been accomplished so far in Thessalonica, Paul desires that the word "spread rapidly" [lit., keep on running] and allow others to share in the glory of God. He also asks for prayers concerning his personal welfare, since "perverse and evil men" continually confront and harass him—those who seek to hinder or malign the gospel of Christ (2 Pet. 2:1–3). "Perverse" usually comes from a word meaning "crooked" or "unreasonable" (as in Acts 2:40 and 1 Pet. 2:18); here the word refers to moral corruption—as in a person that is *not right* (with God). Such is the case with those men (Judaizers and otherwise) who stand opposed to Paul's gospel with Judaism or their self-serving agendas. "For not all have faith"—i.e., not all believe (in the gospel) as the Thessalonian Christians did (1 Thess. 1:9), and this failure to believe is what makes men "preserve and evil." This can also mean "not all are *faithful* (or, have *fidelity*)." Both translations from the Greek are possible, and the commentators seem evenly divided on the matter.[111]

"But the Lord is faithful" (3:3)—i.e., while some resist the truth and therefore are untrustworthy, God is always truthful and dependable. He will not only deliver Paul (Phil. 1:18–20) but also the Thessalonians from their own trials due to their faith (recall 1:3–4; see 1 Thess. 1:6–7). "To say, while praying, 'the Lord is faithful' is another way of uttering the Amen."[112] If indeed the Thessalonians put their full confidence in God and put on the spiritual armor that is divinely provided to them (Eph. 6:10–17, 1 Thess. 5:8), then He "will strengthen and protect you from the evil one." The "evil one" consistently refers to Satan (Mat. 13:19, John 17:15, 1 John 2:13, 5:19, etc.); it is his power and wicked influence that is behind all opposition to God, His gospel, and His ministers.[113] Yet, while

---

111 Compare, for example, Coffman (*Commentary*, 120–121), who argues for "fidelity," and Gloag (*Pulpit Commentary*, 62–63), who argues for "the Christian faith." In my opinion, Paul means here *the* faith, since otherwise it makes little sense to expect "perverse and evil men" to practice fidelity.

112 Bruce, *WBC*, 201.

113 The word *can* be translated simply "evil" here, rather than "the evil one." However, the context portrays evil here in a personal way, and so many Bible translations have "the evil one." In either case, the situation still speaks of Satan and his wicked agenda, since he is the ultimate inspiration for all evil among men.

Satan is indeed more powerful and resourceful than Christians, God is far more powerful and resourceful than Satan. Thus, Paul (again) does not want the Thessalonians to go head-to-head on their own against Satan's ministers, but to rely on God's strength and providence to deliver them.

Having said this, Paul also has confidence that the Thessalonians will do exactly as he has instructed them (3:4; see 1 Thess. 4:1). Paul has not offered them suggestions to follow but commandments to keep; this necessarily implies a transcendent authority, not one that is of men but that comes from God (see Gal. 1:11–12). "May the Lord direct your hearts" (3:5)—now Paul offers a prayer-like appeal to God on behalf of these people. He asks that the Lord remove whatever hindrances stand in their way of full obedience. The "love of God" will condition and provide the correct motive for everything they do (1 Cor. 16:14); the "steadfastness [or, patient endurance] of Christ" refers to Christ's patient appeal for God to take care of Him rather than resort to vengeance or self-reliance (1 Pet. 2:21–23). Paul is saying, "I pray that God will help you to exhibit His love in your own conduct, but you need to let Him take care of those things that lie beyond your ability to control."

Dealing with the "Unruly" (2 Thess. 3:6–15)

Strong Words for Impenitent Brethren (3:6–10): While Paul speaks highly of the Thessalonians overall, even so there are some who are acting irresponsibly toward his teaching on the Second Coming. These latter people are sitting around doing nothing—always at someone else's expense—and waiting for the Lord to appear in the clouds. Such behavior is inappropriate of those who represent Christ. Christians are supposed to be responsible, industrious, and good stewards of their time and resources. In the first epistle, Paul instructed them to "make it your ambition to lead a quiet life and attend to your own business and work with your hands, just as we commanded you, so that you will behave properly toward outsiders and not be in any need" (1 Thess. 4:11). Yet the problem persists, and now he must speak much more strongly and pointedly.

"Now we command you" (3:6)—this is indeed a solemn command, one that cannot be violated or ignored without severe consequences. Paul came to the Thessalonians with gentleness and patience (1 Thess. 2:7–12) but not everyone responds rightly to such noble conduct. Now he needs to assert his authority as an apostle (cp. 1 Thess. 2:6) and he expects to be heard. Commandments of God are not open to discussion; they are to be obeyed, not interpreted—and especially not challenged.[114]

Paul then states the command itself: "keep away [or, avoid; withdraw yourselves from] every brother who leads an unruly life [or, leads an undisciplined life; walks disorderly] and not according to the tradition … from us" (3:6). "Tradition" again refers to the apostolic teaching that Paul received from the Holy Spirit and handed down to the churches (recall 2:15). The Thessalonian Christians are not to tolerate any brother or sister in Christ who refuses to obey this instruction. It is impossible for a congregation to "preserve the unity of the Spirit" (Eph. 4:3) when only some of its members respect and obey the *authority* of the Spirit and the *headship* of Christ.

Thus, separation is necessary: the disorderly and rebellious must be removed from the local group. (This does *not* remove them from Christ's spiritual church, since that is something that Christ alone has the authority to do.) They must remove the corruptive element within the group for the sake of the group's spiritual integrity. "Withdrawal from the disorderly was thus forced upon the true members for their own sakes as well as for a warning to those from whom they were withdrawing."[115]

The NT repeatedly gives instruction to sever fellowship with impenitent people:

---

114 "We" here ("Now we command you") cannot be taken to put Paul, Silvanus, and Timothy on an equal level of authority. It is an editorial "we," not a collective one. Clearly, Paul has been commissioned as an apostle of Jesus Christ (Rom. 1:1, Gal. 1:1, etc.), and nowhere have we seen Silvanus or Timothy being so commissioned, or either one of them being referred to as though they had. Paul simply means, "As an apostle, I command you—and those who are with me will support my decision—to do this thing."

115 Lenski, *Interpretation*, 458.

- ❑ "If your brother sins, go and show him his fault in private; if he listens to you, you have won your brother. But if he does not listen to you, take one or two more with you, so that by the mouth of two or three witnesses every fact may be confirmed. If he refuses to listen to them, tell it to the church; and if he refuses to listen even to the church, let him be to you as a Gentile and a tax collector" (Mat. 18:15–17).
- ❑ "Now I urge you, brethren, keep your eye on those who cause dissensions and hindrances contrary to the teaching which you learned, **and turn away from them**. For such men are slaves, not of our Lord Christ but of their own appetites; and by their smooth and flattering speech they deceive the hearts of the unsuspecting" (Rom. 16:17–18, emphasis added).
- ❑ "I wrote to you not to associate with any so-called brother if he is an immoral person, or covetous, or an idolater, or a reviler, or a drunkard, or a swindler—not even to eat with such a one. . . . Remove the wicked man from among yourselves" (1 Cor. 5:11, 13).
- ❑ "Reject a factious man after a first and second warning, knowing that such a man is perverted and is sinning, being self-condemned" (Titus 3:10–11).
- ❑ "If anyone comes to you and does not bring this teaching, do not receive him into your house, and do not give him a greeting; for the one who gives him a greeting participates in his evil deeds" (2 John 1:10–11).

Such action is seldom easy and must never be taken lightly. "Few things in our churches are more difficult of wise execution than the discipline of erring members."[116]

As an example of positive behavior, Paul reminds the Thessalonians of his and his companions' conduct while they were among them. Just as he (and Silas and Timothy) did not act in an undisciplined manner, so he expects these men and women to "follow our example" (3:7). Specifically, Paul did not quit working and live off others' support while he waited for the Lord to come. Instead, he worked hard to earn his own

116 Robertson, *Word Pictures*, 61.

keep and deliberately tried *not* to become a burden to anyone (3:8; see also Acts 18:1–3 and 2 Cor. 11:7–9).

"Not because we do not have the right to do this" (3:9)—i.e., it *is* the church's responsibility to pay its ministers who preach the gospel for a living (1 Cor. 9:7–14). Paul had every right to be paid for his services, especially given the importance of the work that he did for them. Yet, he voluntarily chose to relinquish this right "in order to offer ourselves as a model for you" (cp. 1 Cor. 9:11–18). In other words, Paul was deserving of compensation, but he declined this; in contrast, these undisciplined people who are sitting around waiting for Christ to return have earned nothing, yet they expect others (including the church) to feed them.

Paul then reminds them of an earlier instruction: "For even when we were with you, we used to give you this order: if anyone is not willing to work, then he is not to eat, either" (3:10).[117] This means if a man chooses to be irresponsible and refuses to support himself, the church is not to provide assistance for him, financial or otherwise. God does not support lazy, undisciplined, or disobedient conduct, no matter what motive or explanation such people give—and neither should His people. Those who are "undisciplined" and idle often meddle in other people's business, gossip, and engage in similar unchristian behavior (3:11). "Busybodies" is from a word that means "to waste one's labor about (a thing)" or "to busy oneself about trifling, needless, useless matters."[118] With the full authority of an apostle of Christ, Paul commands *and* exhorts such people to pay attention to their own affairs, be gainfully employed, and eat their own food (3:12). "Exhort" in this case indicates an urgent pleading, since these people are endangering their own souls with their irresponsible conduct.

An Encouragement to Stay the Course (3:13–15): "But as for you, brethren, do not grow weary of doing good" (3:13). Paul addresses this

117 "This is a saying that Paul picked up and applied to their particular situation. The saying was in common use, appearing in Hebrew in *Bereshith Rabba* and in the book *Zeror*" (JFB, *Commentary* [electronic], on 3:10). Even so, Paul's usage of this saying has made it (by inspiration) part of the biblical text rather than simply a Jewish idiom.

118 *NAS Dictionaries* (electronic); Thayer, *Lexicon* (electronic), G4020. This is a *paronomasia*—a play on words—in the Greek: lit., busy with what is none of their business (Lenski, *Interpretation*, 463).

to those whom the ones sitting around doing nothing productive have taken advantage of. In essence, he says, "Don't let this bad experience sour your desire to do good to those who are truly in need and will be genuinely grateful for your kindness" (see 1 Cor. 15:58, 2 Cor. 4:1, and Gal. 6:9–10).

"If anyone does not obey our instruction [or, word]" (3:14)—twice now Paul has written to this element within the Thessalonian church that has chosen to live irresponsibly. If these people will not listen to apostolic instruction, then they forfeit all fellowship with Christians. It is not possible for one who acts like an unbeliever to live in harmony with believers (2 Cor. 6:14–16). And one who resists Paul resists the One who sent him, namely, Christ (Luke 10:16, in principle; recall 1 Thess. 4:8).

"Take special note of that person" (3:14)—i.e., mark or identify him as one who is no longer welcome as a brother in good standing with the Lord. "And do not associate with him"—i.e., in whatever context that one would normally associate or enjoy spiritual fellowship with a faithful Christian, particularly in the assemblies of believers. The "association" of which Paul speaks has everything to do with *Christian* association. In some cases, this person may be someone's father, husband, or other family member—a physical relationship that simply cannot be avoided.[119] On the other hand, this must also mean that in whatever manner Christians must deal with this person, it cannot be in such a way that overlooks that person's state of rebellion to God.

"Yet do not regard him as an enemy, but admonish him as a brother" (3:15)—i.e., he is not *your* enemy, but is instead a wayward brother (or

119 "In response to a question concerning whether a wife was to eat or otherwise keep company with a husband who has been withdrawn from in light of 1 Cor. 5:11, Guy N. Woods responded as follows: 'It seems clear that Paul was not alluding to a relationship involving husband and wife in the passage cited. The laws of God are never in conflict; all truth is harmonious with itself, and the principles under which God ordains we are to live are never contradictory. Wives have duties to their husbands—whether they are Christians or not—and these duties harmonize with their obligations as Christians, as well. Marriage relationships were designed of God to take precedence over all other relationships; any situation later arising must be understood in light of this fact. The Christian wife should therefore continue to live with her husband and use her influence to bring him to repentance.' We fully concur with his remarks" (Dub McClish, "Corrective Church Discipline," *Studies*, 349).

sister) in Christ. No Christian or group of Christians has authority to revoke one's brotherly status, no matter how far from God that person has strayed. Thus, it is not necessary—or appropriate—to avoid him altogether, but to use whatever opportunities are available to improve his spiritual welfare. In *all* cases of church discipline—and that is exactly what is being discussed here—the desired outcome is *restoration*, not seeking one's destruction.[120] "[S]o that he will be put to shame" identifies the *purpose* for the separation of spiritual fellowship: it cannot be out of spite, vengeance, or indignation; it must be to bring him to a state of repentance and spiritual renewal (Rev. 2:5, 3:3). Once his relationship with God has been restored, then so can his fellowship with believers. Upon such restoration, the congregation is to forgive him and reaffirm their love for him (2 Cor. 2:6–8).

Final Remarks (2 Thess. 3:16–18)

Paul has spoken strongly toward those in sin, but he certainly does not want to end his letter with such a tone (3:16). At the same time, he necessarily implies the *source* of Christians' peace and unity: it must be in "the Lord," and not in one's circle of friends, physical family members, or congregation. People can seek unity in all the wrong things, or for all the wrong reasons; unity *by itself* does not bring about God's peace. Only when people unite *in Christ* can they enjoy peace and fellowship with God. "Lord" here can refer to Christ or the Father, since both are (to us) "the God of peace" (Rom. 15:33, 16:20, 2 Cor. 13:11, and Heb. 13:20), and both Personages are the basis for our peace (Titus 1:4, Phile. 3, 2 Peter 1:2, 2 John 3, etc.). The antecedent of this phrase, however, is "the Lord Jesus Christ" (from 3:6, 12).

120 "Clearly this purpose is reformatory. It springs from love, from the desire to heal, not from the desire to get rid of an individual whom one does not happen to favor" (Hendriksen, *NTC*, 206). But we must also guard against going too far in the other direction. "A dangerous error being witnessed in the church today is that of using 'love' as an excuse for toleration of sin. ... [In such cases,] vital areas of doctrine and practice are neglected because of a woeful misunderstanding of love. ...Disciplinary action toward the 'disorderly brother' is not a demonstration of *absence* of love, but rather the *presence* of genuine love—love for God *and* for the brother walking out of harmony with the body" (Tom Wacaster, "Command to Withdraw and Closing Words," *Studies*, 291–292; emphases are his; bracketed words are mine).

Peace among Christians does not require the absence of conflict in this life, for this is impossible; however, it most certainly refers to having peace *with God* no matter what happens to us in this life (Rom. 5:1–5). Thus, Paul does not say, "May God remove every person or circumstance from you that would threaten your peace in this world," but, "*In Christ*, you can be at peace (or, find contentment) in whatever circumstance you must face" (cp. Phil. 4:11–13, 19).

"I, Paul, write this greeting with my own hand…" (3:17). Paul commonly dictates his letters to an *amanuensis* (or secretary; see Rom. 16:22, for example) but uses his own handwriting to pen the farewell address (1 Cor. 16:21, Gal. 6:11, and Col. 4:18). This provides authenticity to his epistles and distinguishes his genuine letters from any false correspondences (recall 2:1–3). In the present case, Paul goes out of his way to assure the Thessalonians that "this is the way I write"—lit., this is my actual and distinctive handwriting.[121]

"The grace of our Lord Jesus Christ be with you all" (3:18)—a common benediction of Paul's epistles. Notice how often Paul uses this expression "Lord Jesus Christ": fourteen times in the *Thessalonian* letters alone and fifty times in his epistles altogether. Each part of this phrase is critically important: He is **Lord** over all other lords and authorities (Col. 1:15–17); He is **Jesus**, the One who once walked upon this earth and lived a perfect life; and He is the **Christ**, the Son of the living God and Redeemer of humankind (Mat. 16:16, John 20:31). Paul's initial preaching to the Thessalonians was to confirm that Jesus the Man was indeed the Christ (Messiah) of prophecy (Acts 17:1–3). Anyone who denies Jesus' divine nature *as* the Christ (Son of God) makes himself an "antichrist" (1 John 2:22–23, 4:2–3, and 5:10–12). Thus, Paul affirms—fifty times!—in his epistles that Jesus most certainly is "the Christ," the Son of God.

121 "There is no ground for concluding…that Paul's drawing attention to his autograph and signature means that the *whole* of 2 Thessalonians (as of Galatians, 1 Corinthians and Philemon) was written in Paul's hand" (Bruce, *WBC*, 216).

Sources Used for *1 & 2 Thessalonians*:

Barnes, Albert. *Barnes' Notes* (electronic edition). Database © 2014 by WORDsearch Corp. (orig. published in London, 1885).

Bruce, F. F. *Word Biblical Commentary, vol. 45: 1 & 2 Thessalonians.* Nashville: Thomas Nelson, Inc., 1982.

Coffman, James Burton. *Commentary on 1 & 2 Thessalonians, 1 & 2 Timothy, Titus, and Philemon.* Austin, TX: Firm Foundation, 1978.

Cogdill, Roy. *The New Testament: Book by Book.* Marion, IN: Cogdill Foundation Publications, 1975.

Gloag, P. J. "1 Thessalonians" and "2 Thessalonians." *The Pulpit Commentary*, vol. XXI. H. D. M. Spence and Joseph S. Exell, eds. Peabody, MA: Hendrickson Publishers, no date (orig. published late 19th century).

Hailey, Homer. *A Commentary on Daniel: A Prophetic Message.* Las Vegas: Nevada Publications, 2001.

Hendriksen, William and Simon J. Kistemaker. *New Testament Commentary: Thessalonians, the Pastorals, and Hebrews.* Grand Rapids: Baker Books, 1995.

Jamieson, Robert, Andrew R. Fausset, and David Brown. *Jamieson, Fausset, and Brown Commentary: Commentary Critical and Explanatory on the Whole Bible (1871)* (electronic edition). Database © 2012 by WORDsearch Corp.

Lenski, R. C. H. *Commentary on the New Testament: The Interpretation of Paul's Epistles to the Colossians, to the Thessalonians, to Timothy, to Titus, and to Philemon.* Peabody, MA: Hendrickson Publishers, 1998.

Longstreth, Jason S., ed. *A Life Worthy of the Gospel: Studies in the Macedonian Epistles*, Florida College Annual Lectures (2023). Temple Terrace, FL: Florida College Press, 2023.

McClish, Dub (ed.). *Studies in 1 & 2 Thessalonians, Philemon.* Denton, TX: Valid Publications, 1988.

Robertson, A. T. *Word Pictures in the New Testament,* vol. IV. Grand Rapids: Baker Book House, no date (© 1931 by SBC).

Russell, D. S. *Between the Testaments.* Philadelphia: Fortress Press, 1965.

Strong, James. *Strong's Talking Greek-Hebrew Dictionary* (electronic edition). Database © WORDsearch Corp.

Sychtysz, Chad. *The Holy Spirit of God: A Biblical Perspective.* Waynesville, OH: Spiritbuilding Publishers, 2010.

Thayer, Joseph. *Thayer's Greek-English Lexicon* (electronic edition). Database © 2005 WORDsearch Corp.

Thomas, Robert L., ed. *New American Standard Hebrew, Aramaic, and Greek Dictionaries* (electronic edition). © 1998 by The Lockman Foundation.

www.ingramcontent.com/pod-product-compliance
Lightning Source LLC
LaVergne TN
LVHW052338100826
845147LV00020B/1106

* 9 7 8 1 9 6 4 8 0 5 5 1 1 *